CREATIVE CONNECTIONS

USING ART TO EXPLORE SCIENCE IN PRIMARY CLASSROOM

DR MEENAKSHI NARULA

I would like to dedicate this book, **"Creative Connections: Using Art to Explore Science in Primary Classroom"**, to three exceptional individuals who have played a significant role in my journey as an educator.

Firstly, I dedicate this book to my science teacher, whose passion and dedication to science ignited the spark in me to pursue science education. It was under his guidance that I developed a deep love for science, which has continued to inspire me throughout my career.

Secondly, I dedicate this book to my school-time Principal, **Late Mrs. Shashi Prashar Ji**, who was my mentor during my early years as an educator. Her guidance, support, and encouragement have been invaluable to me, and I owe much of my success to her.

Finally, I dedicate this book to **Ms. Anshu Malika Kumar**, a veteran science educator and my mentor, who inspired me to think out of the box and teach creatively. Her innovative approach to science education and her commitment to excellence has been a constant source of inspiration for me, and I am grateful for the impact she has had on my career.

To these three exceptional individuals, I offer my heartfelt gratitude and dedicate this book as a token of appreciation for the invaluable role they have played in my journey as an educator.

Contents

Preface   *xiii*

  1. Learning By Doing   1

  2. Bringing Science To Life   2

  3. Becoming Science   3

  4. Engaging In Scientific Dialogue   4

  5. Asking The Right Questions   5

  6. Discovering Science   6

  7. Collaborating For Science   7

  8. Visualizing Science   8

  9. Applying Science   9

10. Experiencing Science Online   10

11. Connecting Science   11

12. Thinking Scientifically   12

13. Playing For Science   13

14. Seeing Science In Action   14

15. Visualizing Science Concepts   15

16. Teaching And Learning Together   16

17. Telling Science Tales   17

18. Solving Scientific Problems   18

19. Organizing Science   19

20. Building Scientific Models   20

21. Sharing Science Ideas   21

22. Collaborating For Scientific Understanding   22

23. Building Science Skills Step By Step   23

24. Flipping Science Learning   24

25. Interactive Science Teaching   25

26. Changing Scientific Perspectives   26

27. Teaching Science For All   27

Contents

28. Learning Science On Your Own   28

29. Acting Out Science Concepts   29

30. Working Together For Science   30

31. Investigating Science   31

32. Cooperating For Science   32

33. Mapping Science Connections   33

34. Arguing For Science Understanding   34

35. Simulating Science Experiments   35

36. Playing For Science Understanding   36

37. Solving Science Mysteries   37

38. Seeing Science Concepts   38

39. Cartooning Science Concepts   39

40. Learning Science Through Play   40

41. Reflecting On Science Learning   41

42. Collaborating For Inquiry Learning   42

43. Changing Science Perspectives   43

44. Exploring Science From Afar   44

45. Getting Hands-on With Science   45

46. Modeling Science Concepts   46

47. Challenging Students To Stem   47

48. Teaching Science To Learn Science   49

49. Designing Solutions For Science   50

50. Projecting Science Learning   51

51. Socratically Questioning Science   52

52. Blogging For Science Literacy   53

53. Journalistically Exploring Science   54

54. Debating Science Issues   55

55. Science For The People   56

Contents

56. Researching Science Together   58

57. Comic Science   59

58. Podcasting Science   60

59. Journalistically Reporting Science   61

60. Augmenting Science Learning   62

61. Improv-ing Science   63

62. Animating Science   64

63. Theater For Science Learning   65

64. Puzzling Out Science   66

65. Art For Science Learning   67

66. Mindful Science Learning   68

67. Science Through Time   69

68. Science In Stories   70

69. Writing Science   71

70. Math In Science   72

71. Artistic Science   74

72. Science And Society   75

73. Fitness And Science   76

74. Coding Science   78

75. Science Of The Earth   79

76. Science Of Money   81

77. Science Memory Lane   82

78. Science Comprehension Quest   83

79. Science Application Workshop   84

80. Science Analysis Lab   85

81. Science Evaluation Panel   86

82. Science Creation Studio   87

83. Science Storytelling   88

Contents

84. Science Simulation Lab — 89

85. Science Debate Club — 90

86. Science Invention Competition — 91

87. Science Debate For Sustainable Development — 92

88. Science Problem-solving Challenge — 93

89. Science Design Challenge — 94

90. Science Songs For Sustainability — 95

91. Science Hands-on Lab — 96

92. Science Collaborative Projects — 97

93. Science Reflection Journals — 98

94. Science Nature Exploration — 99

95. Science Ethics And Values Discussions — 100

96. Science Project-based Learning — 101

97. Collaborative Idea Generation — 102

98. Observation And Inquiry — 104

99. Metacognitive Reflection — 106

100. Empathy And Perspective-taking — 107

101. Evidence-based Reasoning — 108

102. Building On Prior Knowledge — 109

103. Visual Thinking — 110

104. Making Connections And Summarizing — 111

105. Summarizing And Synthesizing — 112

106. Silent Brainstorming — 114

107. Empathy And Perspective-taking — 115

108. Observation And Detail — 116

109. Close Reading And Analysis — 117

110. Evidence-based Reasoning And Argumentation — 118

111. Exploring Different Perspectives — 119

Contents

112. Evidence-based Reasoning And Explanation 121

113. Vocabulary And Concept Development 122

114. Critical Thinking And Problem-solving 123

115. Change Over Time And Historical Thinking 124

116. Persuasive Argumentation And Debate 126

117. Understanding Different Perspectives 127

118. Understanding Systems And Relationships 129

119. Building Connections And Expanding Thinking 130

120. Observation And Inquiry 131

121. Summarizing And Synthesizing Information 132

122. Asking Effective Questions 133

123. Collaborative Thinking And Sharing 134

124. Reflecting And Revising Thinking 136

125. Generating And Sharing Ideas 138

126. Reflecting On Learning And Growth 140

127. Plant A Seed, Watch It Grow: Discover The Wonders Of Plant Life! 142

128. From Furry Friends To Fierce Predators: Explore The Diversity Of Animal Life! 148

129. Healthy Habits For A Happy Body: Exploring The Wonders Of Human Health And Hygiene! 152

130. Rock Your World: Discovering The Magic Of Rocks, Salts, And Minerals! 158

131. Breath Of Life: Exploring The Vital Importance Of Air And Water To Our Planet! 162

132. Power Up: Discovering The Wonders Of Force, Work, And Energy! 165

133. Beyond The Horizon: Discovering The Wonders Of Heavenly Bodies, Space, And The Universe! 169

134. Protecting Our Home: Discovering The Importance Of Saving And 174

Contents

Preserving Our Environment!

135. Dress To Impress, Every Day	177
136. Matter Matters - In All Its States!	180
137. Precision Counts, Measure Twice	183
138. Home Is Where The Heart Is, No Matter The Type	185
139. Illuminate Your World, Amplify Your Voice	188
140. Birds Of A Feather, With Beaks That Flock Together	190
141. Seasons Change, But The Weather Remains	193
142. Safety First, Care Always	196
143. Details On Some Activities/experiments	198

Dancing Raisins

Oobleck Experiment

Jello Sensory Play

Marshmallow Molecules

Magnetic Putty

Frozen Paint Art

Bean Bag Toss

Monopoly House Building

Musical Painting

Musical Water Glasses

Bird Watching Bingo

Weather Bingo

Safety Diorama

144. Project 1: Plant A Garden For A Sustainable Future	225
145. Project 2: Wild Adventures	230
146. Project 3: Climate Crusaders	234
147. Project 4: Foodies Unite	238
148. Project 5: Birds Of India	243

Contents

149. Project 6: Threads Of Diversity   248

150. Eliciting Evidence Of Learning   254

151. Activating Students' Prior Knowledge   257

152. Activating Learners As Owners Of Their Learning   260

153. The Feedback That Moves Learning Forward   263

154. Learning Intentions   267

155. Learning Ladder   272

End Note   275

Preface

As an educator and a science enthusiast, I firmly believe that science is not just a subject to be taught, but a way of thinking and exploring the world around us. However, the traditional methods of teaching science often fail to capture the interest and imagination of young minds. It is here that the integration of art and science can work wonders in making science more accessible, engaging, and fun for young learners.

With this belief in mind, I am delighted to present my latest book, **"Creative Connections: Using Art to Explore Science in Primary Classroom"**. This book is a sequel to my earlier book **"Artful Science"**, which focused on integrating art and science at the middle school level. In this book, I have extended my ideas and strategies to the primary level to help teachers engage their students in scientific exploration and discovery through the creative medium of art.

The main objective of this book is to help teachers create a learning environment that fosters scientific thinking, creativity, and curiosity in young learners. By using art to explore science, teachers can not only make science more interesting and enjoyable but also help students develop a deeper understanding of scientific concepts and their real-life applications.

The book is divided into chapters that cover various science topics as per Primary School Curriculum. Each chapter provides a range of art-based activities that teachers can use to reinforce scientific concepts and encourage students to think critically and creatively. The activities are designed to be hands-on, interactive, and adaptable to different learning styles and abilities.

In conclusion, I hope that this book will inspire teachers to explore the exciting possibilities of integrating art and science in their classrooms and help them create a learning environment that encourages scientific thinking, creativity, and innovation. I also hope that this book will help students develop a love for science and a lifelong curiosity about the world around them.

Dr. Meenakshi Narula

1

Learning By Doing

Learning By Doing

Hands-on experiments - "Learning by Doing"

Students learn through active participation in experiments that allow them to apply scientific concepts and theories to real-world situations.

For example, students can build and launch rockets to learn about the laws of motion.

2
Bringing Science to Life

Bringing Science to Life

Field trips - "Bringing Science to Life"
Students engage in experiential learning outside the classroom, gaining firsthand experience of scientific phenomena.

For example, a field trip to a museum or zoo can help students understand animal adaptations.

3

Becoming Science

Becoming Science

Role-playing - "Becoming Science"
Students take on the roles of scientists, historians, or other professionals to learn about scientific discoveries and developments.

For example, students can role-play a scientific debate about the origin of the universe.

4

Engaging in Scientific Dialogue

"Engaging in Scientific Dialogue"

Debate - "Engaging in Scientific Dialogue"
Students argue for or against a particular scientific viewpoint, helping them develop critical thinking and communication skills.

For example, students can debate the benefits and drawbacks of genetically modified foods.

5
Asking the Right Questions

Asking the Right Questions

Socratic questioning - "Asking the Right Questions"
The teacher asks open-ended questions to help students develop critical thinking skills and analyze scientific concepts.

For example, students can explore the ethical implications of cloning through Socratic questioning.

6

Discovering Science

Discovering Science

Inquiry-based learning - "Discovering Science"
Students investigate scientific concepts through their own observations and questions, developing problem-solving and critical thinking skills.

For example, students can design and conduct experiments to determine the factors that affect plant growth.

7
Collaborating for Science

Collaborating for Science

Collaborative group work - "Collaborating for Science"
Students work together to solve scientific problems, developing teamwork and communication skills.

For example, students can work in groups to build a model of the human digestive system.

8

Visualizing Science

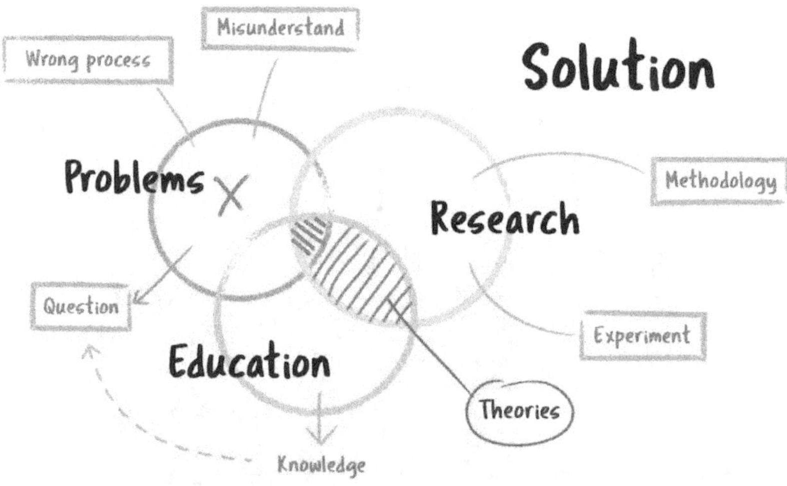

Visualizing Science

Concept mapping - "Visualizing Science"
Students create visual representations of scientific concepts and their relationships, aiding in understanding and recall.

For example, students can create a concept map of the different types of energy and how they are transformed.

9
Applying Science

Applying Science

Project-based learning - "Applying Science"
Students work on long-term projects that involve applying scientific concepts to real-world situations, and developing research and problem-solving skills.

For example, students can design a sustainable energy plan for their school.

10

Experiencing Science Online

Experiencing Science Online

Virtual lab simulations - "Experiencing Science Online"
Students use virtual simulations to perform experiments, practice lab skills, and collect data in a safe and controlled environment.
For example, students can use a virtual lab to learn about cell division.

11

Connecting Science

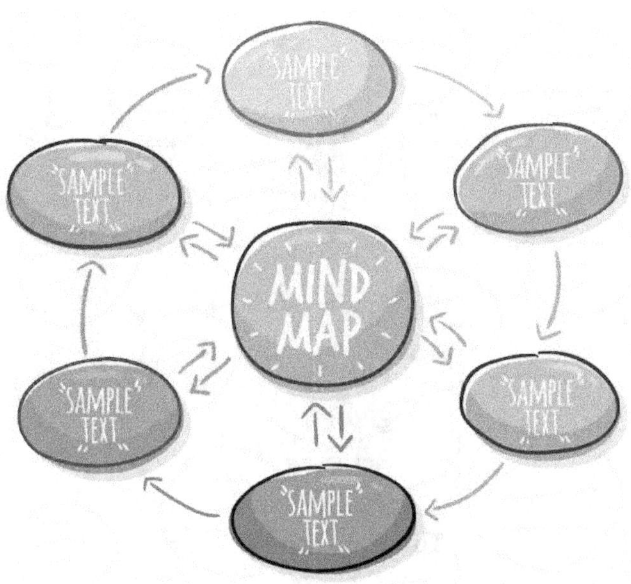

Connecting Science

Mind maps - "Connecting Science"
Students create diagrams that show the relationships between scientific concepts, helping them make connections and organize information.

For example, students can create a mind map of the different biomes and the animals that live in each.

12
Thinking Scientifically

Thinking Scientifically

Critical thinking exercises - "Thinking Scientifically".

Students practice evaluating and analyzing scientific information to develop critical thinking skills.

For example, students can analyze and compare different sources of information about climate change.

13
Playing for Science

Playing for Science

Game-based learning - "Playing for Science"
Students engage in educational games that help them learn scientific concepts and problem-solving skills. For example, students can play a game that simulates the process of natural selection.

14

Seeing Science in Action

Seeing Science in Action

Demonstrations - "Seeing Science in Action"
The teacher shows students how scientific concepts work through live demonstrations, helping them understand complex ideas.
For example, students can watch a demonstration of chemical reactions.

15

Visualizing Science Concepts

Visualizing Science Concepts

Lecture with visuals - "Visualizing Science Concepts"
The teacher presents scientific concepts using visual aids, making the material more engaging and accessible.

For example, the teacher can use diagrams and videos to explain the water cycle.

Students can watch videos that explain the behavior of different chemicals in a lab.

16
Teaching and Learning Together

Teaching and Learning Together

Peer teaching - "Teaching and Learning Together"
Students teach and learn from one another, deepening their understanding of scientific concepts and building communication skills.

For example, students can take turns teaching one another about different ecosystems.

17
Telling Science Tales

Telling Science Tales

Storytelling - "Telling Science Tales"
The teacher or students tell stories that illustrate scientific concepts and processes, making them more memorable and engaging.

For example, students can create stories that explain the water cycle.

18

Solving Scientific Problems

Solving Scientific Problems

Problem-based learning - "Solving Scientific Problems"
Students learn scientific concepts by solving real-world problems and developing critical thinking and problem-solving skills.

For example, students can design a device that uses solar power to purify water.

19
Organizing Science

Organizing Science

Graphic organizers - "Organizing Science"
Students use visual aids such as flowcharts and diagrams to organize scientific concepts, improving understanding and retention.

For example, students can create a graphic organizer that shows the different steps of the scientific method.

20

Building Scientific Models

Building Scientific Models

Model building - "Building Scientific Models"
Students build physical or virtual models of scientific phenomena, helping them understand complex concepts.

For example, students can build creative models on any science concept on their own hypothesis. Also, to start with they can follow their mento's instructions or refer to teaxtbook and gradually build on their own concepts and observations.

21
Sharing Science Ideas

Sharing Science Ideas

Think-pair-share activities - "Sharing Science Ideas"
Students work in pairs or small groups to discuss and share ideas about scientific concepts, improving communication and teamwork skills.

For example, students can discuss and share their ideas about the causes of climate change.

22

Collaborating for Scientific Understanding

Collaborating for Scientific Understanding

Jigsaw activities - "Collaborating for Scientific Understanding"

Students work in small groups to learn about different parts of a scientific concept, and then teach the rest of the class what they have learned, developing teamwork and communication skills.

For example, students can learn about different types of clouds and then teach their classmates.

23

Building Science Skills Step by Step

Building Science Skills Step by Step

Scaffolding techniques - "Building Science Skills Step by Step"
The teacher provides support and guidance to students as they learn scientific concepts, gradually reducing support as students become more independent learners.

For example, the teacher can provide step-by-step guidance as students learn to use a microscope.

24

Flipping Science Learning

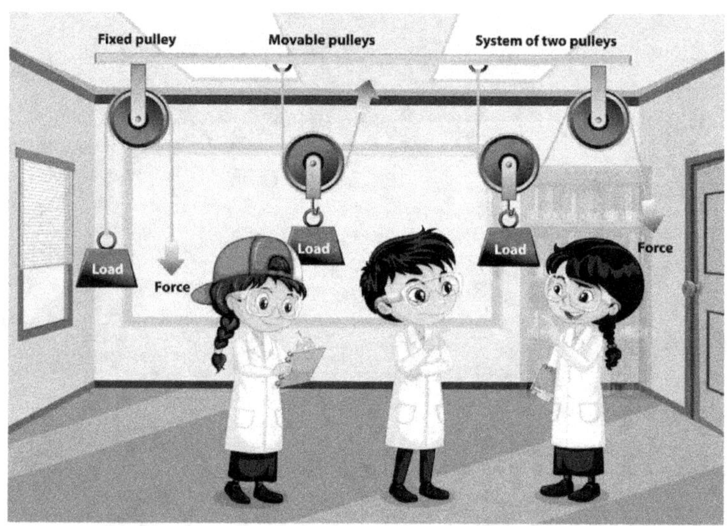

Flipping Science Learning

Flipped classroom approach - "Flipping Science Learning"

Students watch instructional videos or complete readings at home and then work on projects and activities in class, allowing for more hands-on learning and engagement.

For example, students can watch a video about the properties of water at home and then conduct experiments in class.

They can read and explore different types of pulleys in the surroundings and experiment in the class.

25

Interactive Science Teaching

Interactive Science Teaching

Interactive whiteboards - "Interactive Science Teaching"
The teacher uses an interactive whiteboard to engage students and present scientific concepts in an interactive and dynamic way.

For example, the teacher can use an interactive whiteboard to create a virtual lab simulation.

26
Changing Scientific Perspectives

Changing Scientific Perspectives

Conceptual change strategies - "Changing Scientific Perspectives"
The teacher helps students challenge their preconceived ideas about scientific concepts and develop new, more accurate understandings.

For example, the teacher can use activities that challenge students' misconceptions about the properties of matter and other relevant concepts.

27

Teaching Science for All

Differentiated instruction

Differentiated instruction - "Teaching Science for All"
The teacher tailors instruction to meet the diverse learning needs of students, ensuring that every student has access to scientific concepts and experiences.

For example, the teacher can provide different levels of support for students with different learning needs during a lab experiment.

28

Learning Science on Your Own

Learning Science on Your Own

Self-directed learning - "Learning Science on Your Own"
Students take responsibility for their own learning, setting their own learning goals and pace, and pursuing their interests in science.

For example, students can choose their own topics for research and the way of presentation. They can set rubrics on their own under the mentorship of their teacher.

29
Acting Out Science Concepts

Acting Out Science Concepts

Role-playing - "Acting Out Science Concepts"
Students take on different roles and act out scientific concepts, helping them understand complex ideas and processes.

For example, students can role-play on different eating habits of animals, plants, parts of cells etc.

30

Working Together for Science

Working Together for Science

Collaborative projects - "Working Together for Science"
Students work in small groups to complete projects that require research, critical thinking, and problem-solving skills, developing teamwork and communication skills.

For example, students can research and create a presentation about the impact of climate change on ecosystems.

31

Investigating Science

Investigating Science

Inquiry-based learning - "Investigating Science"
Students develop scientific skills by posing questions, conducting experiments, and making observations, developing critical thinking and problem-solving skills.

For example, students can design and conduct an experiment to test the effects of different types of soil on plant growth.

32
Cooperating for Science

Cooperating for Science

Cooperative learning - "Cooperating for Science"
Students work in small groups to complete tasks, developing teamwork and communication skills while learning scientific concepts.

For example, students can work together to research and present on different forms of renewable energy.

33
Mapping Science Connections

Mapping Science Connections

Concept mapping - "Mapping Science Connections"

Students use mind maps to connect and organize scientific concepts, developing a deeper understanding of scientific concepts and relationships. They create visual representations of the relationships between scientific concepts, improving understanding and retention of scientific ideas.

For example, students can create a mind map that shows the relationships between different forms of energy. They can create a concept map that shows the different types of energy and how they are related.

34

Arguing for Science Understanding

Arguing for Science Understanding

Argumentation - "Arguing for Science Understanding"
Students debate and defend scientific ideas, developing critical thinking and communication skills and deepening their understanding of scientific concepts.

For example, students can debate the merits of different approaches to solving the problem of plastic pollution.

35

Simulating Science Experiments

Simulating Science Experiments

Online simulations - "Simulating Science Experiments"
Students use online simulations to conduct virtual experiments, developing scientific skills and understanding without the need for expensive equipment.

For example, students can use an online simulation to experiment with different types of collisions.

36

Playing for Science Understanding

Playing for Science Understanding

Gamification - "Playing for Science Understanding"
Students learn scientific concepts through games, increasing engagement and motivation while developing scientific skills.

For example, students can play a game that teaches the basics of the scientific method.

37

Solving Science Mysteries

Solving Science Mysteries

Mystery activities - "Solving Science Mysteries"
Students solve science-related mysteries, developing critical thinking and problem-solving skills while learning scientific concepts.

For example, students can investigate the mystery of the disappearing bees and develop hypotheses to explain the phenomenon.

38

Seeing Science Concepts

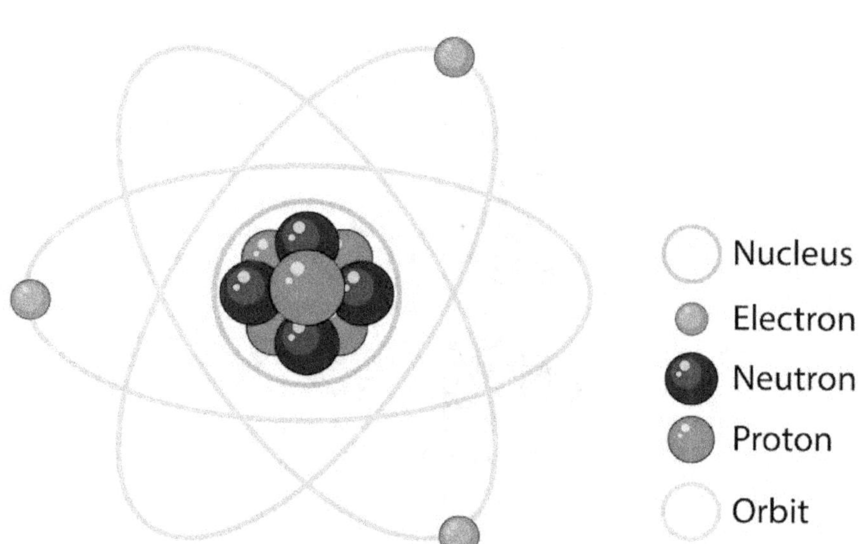

Seeing Science Concepts

Visual aids - "Seeing Science Concepts"

The teacher uses visual aids such as diagrams, charts, and images to help students understand scientific concepts, improving retention and understanding.

For example, the teacher can use a diagram to explain the structure of the atom.

39

Cartooning Science Concepts

Cartooning Science Concepts

Concept cartoons - "Cartooning Science Concepts"

Students create cartoons that illustrate scientific concepts, developing creativity and communication skills while deepening their understanding of scientific ideas.

For example, students can create a cartoon that illustrates the process of photosynthesis.

They can develop their own concept cartoons on any of the given topics as per their curriculum and even beyond.

40
Learning Science Through Play

Learning Science Through Play

Game-based learning - "Learning Science Through Play"
Students learn scientific concepts through games, increasing engagement and motivation while developing scientific skills.

For example, students can play a game that teaches the basics of genetics.

41

Reflecting on Science Learning

Reflecting on Science Learning

Reflective journals - "Reflecting on Science Learning"

Students write reflective journals about their learning experiences, deepening their understanding of scientific concepts and processes while developing critical thinking and communication skills.

For example, students can write a reflective journal entry about their experience conducting a lab experiment.

42

Collaborating for Inquiry Learning

Inquiry Circles

Inquiry circles - "Collaborating for Inquiry Learning"

Students work in small groups to pose and investigate scientific questions, developing scientific skills and communication skills while learning scientific concepts.

For example, students can form an inquiry circle to investigate the impact of water pollution on local ecosystems.

43

Changing Science Perspectives

Changing Science Perspectives

Conceptual change strategies - "Changing Science Perspectives"
Students are taught strategies to challenge and change their preconceived ideas about scientific concepts, developing critical thinking and problem-solving skills while deepening their understanding of scientific concepts.

For example, students can be taught how to identify and challenge misconceptions about climate change.

44

Exploring Science from Afar

Exploring Science from Afar

Virtual field trips - "Exploring Science from Afar"

Students take virtual field trips to explore scientific concepts and phenomena, developing scientific skills and knowledge without leaving the classroom.

For example, students can take a virtual field trip to a coral reef to study the impact of ocean acidification.

45

Getting Hands-on with Science

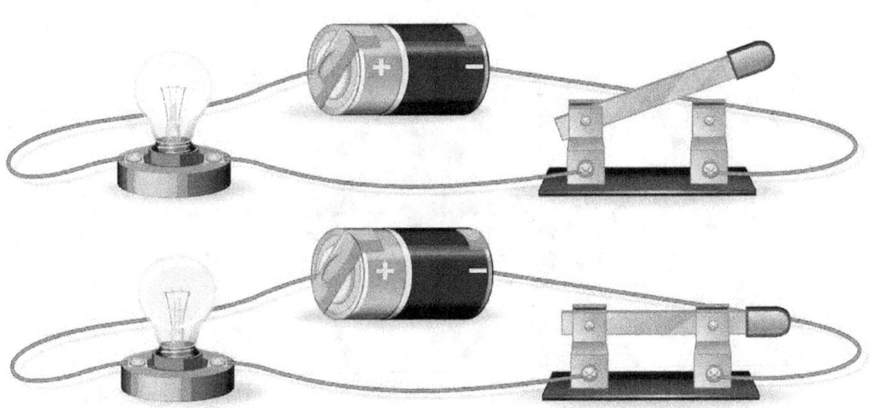

Getting Hands-on with Science

Hands-on activities - "Getting Hands-on with Science"
Students engage in hands-on activities such as experiments and demonstrations to deepen their understanding of scientific concepts and processes.

For example, students can build a simple circuit to learn about electricity.

46

Modeling Science Concepts

Modeling Science Concepts

Model-based learning - "Modeling Science Concepts"
Students use physical or virtual models to represent scientific concepts, developing a deeper understanding and critical thinking skills.

For example, students can use a model of the solar system to learn about planetary motion.

47

Challenging Students to STEM

Challenging Students to STEM

STEM challenges - "Challenging Students to STEM"

Students are challenged to use science, technology, engineering, and math skills to solve real-world problems, developing critical thinking and problem-solving skills while deepening their understanding of scientific concepts.

For example, students can be challenged to design and build a sustainable greenhouse.

Also, a step ahead moving from STEM-STEAM-STREAM you can add Art and Reading/wRiting also for a deeper and holistic 360-degree learning experience.

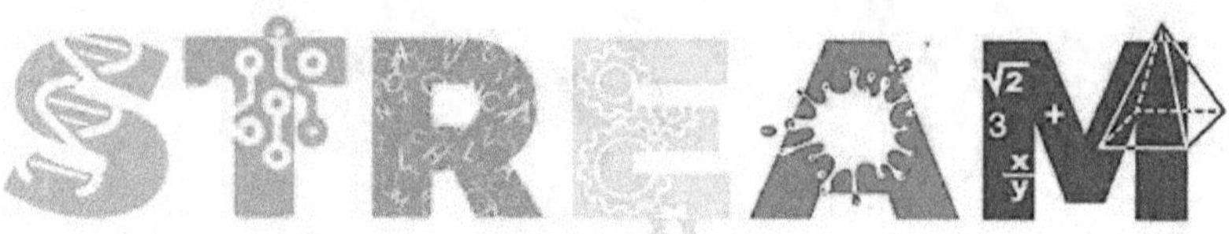

STEM to STREAM (360-degree Learning)

48

Teaching Science to Learn Science

Teaching Science to Learn Science

Peer teaching - "Teaching Science to Learn Science"
Students take turns teaching each other scientific concepts, developing communication and leadership skills while deepening their understanding of scientific concepts.

For example, students can teach each other about the structure of the atom.

49

Designing Solutions for Science

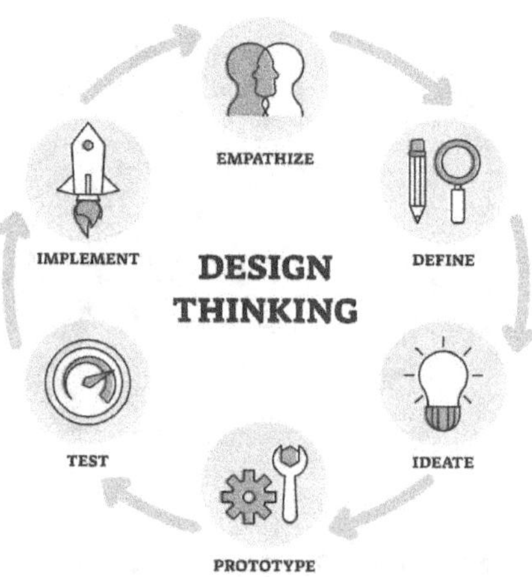

Designing Solutions for Science

Design thinking - "Designing Solutions for Science"
Students use the design thinking process to solve real-world problems related to science, developing critical thinking and problem-solving skills while deepening their understanding of scientific concepts.

For example, students can design a device that uses renewable energy to power a household appliance.

50
Projecting Science Learning

Projecting Science Learning

Project-based learning - "Projecting Science Learning"

Students work collaboratively on a project that involves researching and solving a scientific problem, developing critical thinking, communication, and teamwork skills while deepening their understanding of scientific concepts.

For example, students can work on a project that investigates the impact of pollution on local water sources.

51
Socratically Questioning Science

Socratically Questioning Science

Socratic seminars - "Socratically Questioning Science"
Students engage in a guided discussion where they ask and answer questions about scientific concepts, developing critical thinking and communication skills while deepening their understanding of scientific concepts.

For example, students can participate in a Socratic seminar about the ethics of genetic engineering.

52
Blogging for Science Literacy

Blogging for Science Literacy

Science blogging - "Blogging for Science Literacy"
Students write and publish blog posts about scientific concepts and phenomena, developing research, writing, and communication skills while deepening their understanding of scientific concepts.

For example, students can write a blog post about the impact of deforestation on local ecosystems.

53

Journalistically Exploring Science

Journalistically Exploring Science

Science journalism - "Journalistically Exploring Science"
Students research and write articles about scientific concepts and phenomena, developing research, writing, and communication skills while deepening their understanding of scientific concepts.

For example, students can write an article about the latest scientific research on climate change.

54

Debating Science Issues

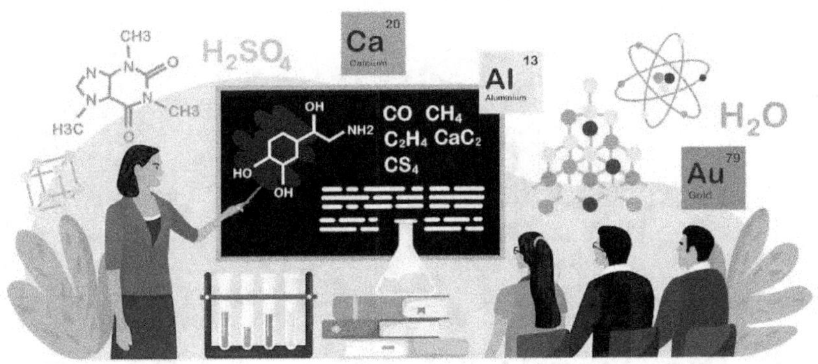

Debating Science Issues

Debate - "Debating Science Issues"

Students engage in a debate about scientific issues, developing critical thinking, communication, and argumentation skills while deepening their understanding of scientific concepts.

For example, students can debate the pros and cons of using nuclear power as an energy source.

55
Science for the People

Science for the People

Citizen science - "Science for the People"
Students participate in real scientific research projects as citizen scientists, developing research, data analysis, and communication skills while contributing to scientific knowledge.

For example, students can participate in a citizen science project that involves monitoring the migration patterns of birds. They can also research on agricultutal best practices and work for the benefit of farmers.

56
Researching Science Together

Researching Science Together

Collaborative research - "Researching Science Together"
Students work collaboratively on a research project that involves conducting experiments, collecting data, and analyzing results, developing critical thinking, communication, and teamwork skills while deepening their understanding of scientific concepts.

For example, students can work together to design and conduct an experiment that investigates the effects of different types of soil on plant growth

57
Comic Science

Comic Science

Science comics - "Comic Science"

Students create and read comics that explain scientific concepts and phenomena, developing creativity, visual literacy, and scientific understanding.

For example, students can create a comic that explains the water cycle.

58
Podcasting Science

Podcasting Science

Science podcasts - "Podcasting Science"

Students create and listen to podcasts that discuss scientific concepts and phenomena, developing research, writing, and communication skills while deepening their understanding of scientific concepts.

For example, students can create a podcast that explores the latest scientific discoveries in genetics.

59
Journalistically Reporting Science

Science Reporters

Citizen journalism - "Journalistically Reporting Science"

Students research and write news articles about scientific discoveries and controversies, developing research, writing, and communication skills while deepening their understanding of scientific concepts.

For example, students can write an article about the impact of plastic pollution on marine ecosystems.

60
Augmenting Science Learning

Augmenting Science Learning

Augmented reality - "Augmenting Science Learning"
Students use augmented reality technology to explore scientific concepts and phenomena in a 3D, interactive environment, developing digital literacy and scientific understanding.

For example, students can use an AR app to explore the human digestive system.

61

Improv-ing Science

Improv-ing Science

Science improv - "Improv-ing Science"

Students participate in improv exercises that involve using scientific concepts and terminology, developing creativity, communication, and scientific understanding.

For example, students can play an improv game where they act out different stages of the water cycle.

62
Animating Science

Animating Science

Science animation - "Animating Science"

Students create animations that explain scientific concepts and phenomena, developing creativity, digital literacy, and scientific understanding.

For example, students can create an animation that explains how sound waves travel through the ear.

63

Theater for Science Learning

Theater for Science Learning

Science Theater - "Theater for Science Learning"
Students participate in theater exercises that involve using scientific concepts and terminology, developing creativity, communication, and scientific understanding.

For example, students can write and perform a play that explains the process of photosynthesis, plant and animal world and many more.

64
Puzzling Out Science

Puzzling Out Science

Science puzzles - "Puzzling Out Science"
Students solve puzzles that involve scientific concepts and phenomena, developing critical thinking, problem-solving, and scientific understanding.

For example, students can solve a crossword puzzle that uses scientific terminology related to climate change.

65

Art for Science Learning

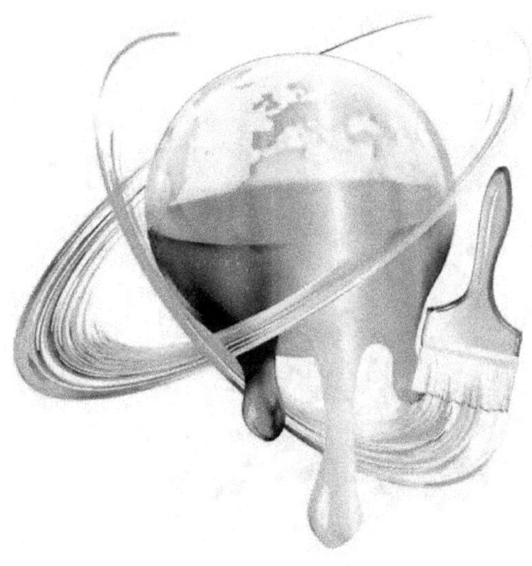

Art for Science Learning

Science art - "Art for Science Learning"

Students create artworks that represent scientific concepts and phenomena, developing creativity, visual literacy, and scientific understanding.

For example, students can create a painting that represents the water cycle.

66

Mindful Science Learning

Mindful Science Learning

Science mindfulness - "Mindful Science Learning"
Students practice mindfulness exercises that involve observing and reflecting on scientific concepts and phenomena, developing attention, awareness, and scientific understanding.

For example, students can practice mindful breathing while observing and reflecting on the process of photosynthesis.

67
Science Through Time

Science Through Time

Science and history - "Science Through Time"

Students explore the history of science, discovering how scientific knowledge has evolved over time, and how it has shaped history.

For example, students can research and present on how ancient civilizations like the Egyptians and Greeks used science to understand the world around them.

68
Science in Stories

Science in Stories

Science and literature - "Science in Stories"

Students analyze how science and technology are represented in literature, exploring how authors use science to comment on society and culture.

For example, students can read and discuss the literature which critiques the ethics of scientific research.

69

Writing Science

Writing Science

Science and language arts - "Writing Science"

Students write creative stories or poems that incorporate scientific concepts and terminology, developing creative writing skills while deepening their understanding of science.

For example, students can write a science fiction story that explores the implications of human genetic engineering.

70
Math in Science

Math in Science

Science and math - "Math in Science"
Students use mathematical concepts to understand scientific phenomena, developing critical thinking and problem-solving skills.

For example, students can use algebra to analyze the relationship between temperature and pressure in a gas.

71
Artistic Science

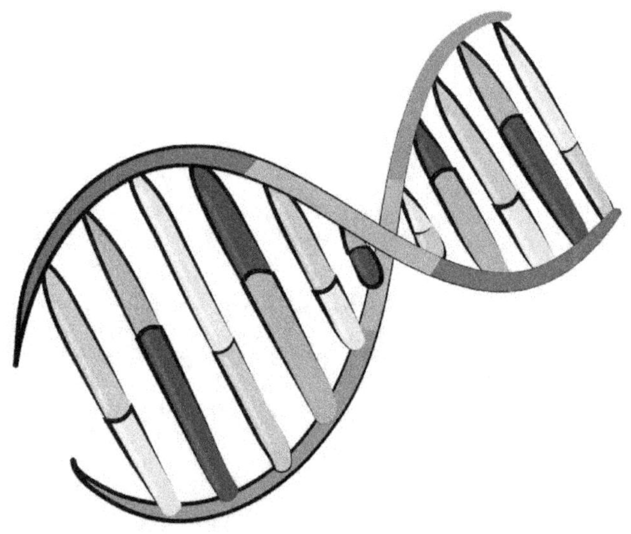

Artistic Science

Science and art - "Artistic Science"
Students use art to represent scientific concepts and phenomena, developing visual literacy and creativity.

For example, students can create a sculpture that represents the structure of DNA.

72
Science and Society

Science and Society

Science and social studies - "Science and Society"

Students analyze how scientific research and technology affect society, developing critical thinking and citizenship skills.

For example, students can research the environmental impacts of using fossil fuels and propose solutions for transitioning to renewable energy.

73
Fitness and Science

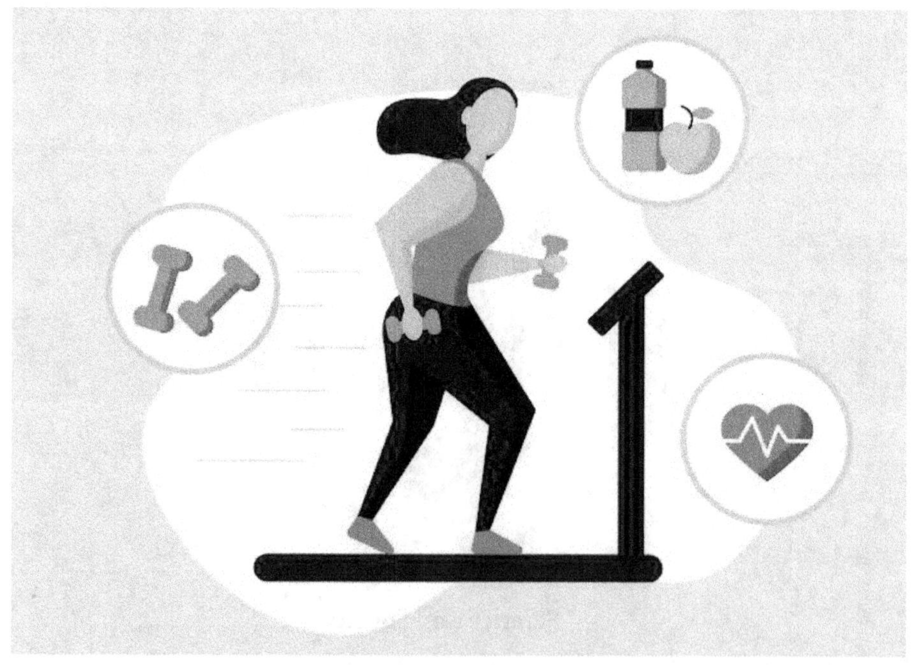

Fitness and Science

Science and physical education - "Fitness and Science"
Students explore how physical exercise affects the human body, developing scientific knowledge and physical fitness.

For example, students can measure their heart rate before and after a workout and analyze how exercise affects their cardiovascular system.

74

Coding Science

Coding Science

Science and computer science - "Coding Science"

Students use computer programming to simulate and model scientific phenomena, developing computational thinking and scientific understanding.

For example, students can code a simulation of the solar system to explore the relative motions of planets.

75
Science of the Earth

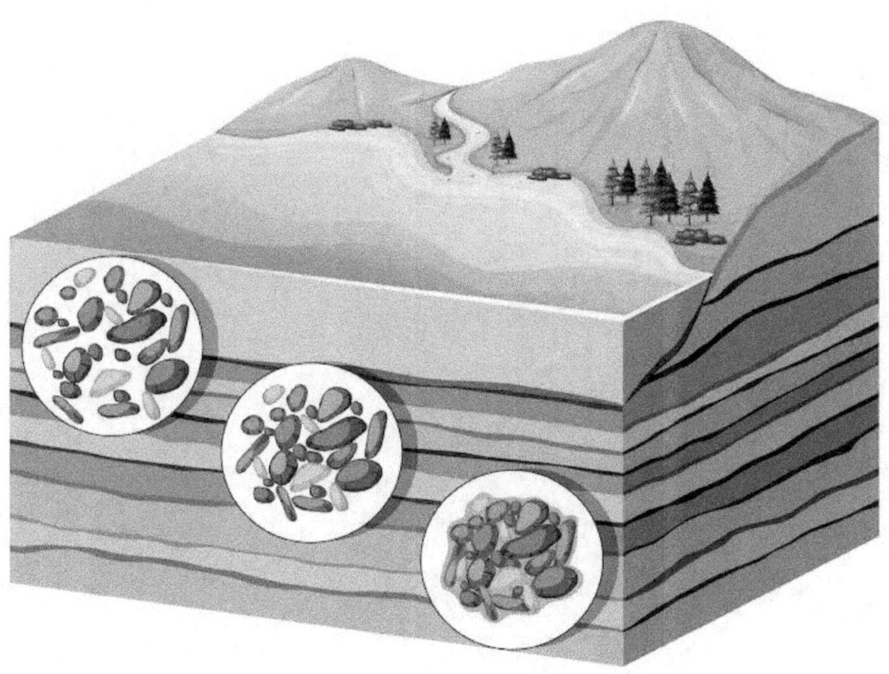

Science of the Earth

Science and geography - "Science of the Earth"
Students explore the physical and environmental aspects of the planet,
developing scientific knowledge and geographical literacy.

For example, students can study plate tectonics and how it affects the formation of mountains and earthquakes.

76
Science of Money

Science of Money

Science and economics - "Science of Money"
Students analyze how scientific research and technology affect the economy, developing critical thinking and financial literacy.

For example, students can research the economic benefits and costs of transitioning to renewable energy.

77

Science Memory Lane

Science Memory Lane

Remembering - "Science Memory Lane"

Students use rote memorization techniques to recall key scientific concepts and terms.

For example, students can use flashcards to memorize the periodic table of elements.

78
Science Comprehension Quest

Science Comprehension Quest

Understanding - "Science Comprehension Quest"
Students analyze and interpret scientific information to develop a deeper understanding of scientific concepts.

For example, students can read and discuss a scientific article on the impacts of climate change on ecosystems.

79

Science Application Workshop

Science Application Workshop

Applying - "Science Application Workshop"

Students use scientific concepts and knowledge to solve real-world problems.

For example, students can design and build a model wind turbine to generate electricity. This is just to start with. They should empathize with the problems in their surroundings and devise their own solutions after applying their knowledge and understanding of concepts.

80
Science Analysis Lab

Science Analysis Lab

Analyzing - "Science Analysis Lab"
Students break down scientific information into smaller parts to analyze and understand how it works.

For example, students can analyze the different components of DNA and how they interact with each other.

81
Science Evaluation Panel

Science Evaluation Panel

Evaluating - "Science Evaluation Panel"
Students evaluate scientific arguments and evidence to determine their validity and reliability.

For example, students can evaluate different scientific studies on the safety and effectiveness of new medicine.

82

Science Creation Studio

Science Creation Studio

Creating - "Science Creation Studio"
Students use scientific knowledge and creativity to develop new ideas and products.

For example, students can design and create a new type of solar-powered device that addresses a specific need in their community.

83
Science Storytelling

Science Storytelling

Remembering/Understanding - "Science Storytelling"

Students use storytelling techniques to remember and understand scientific concepts.

For example, students can create a story or comic strip that explains the process of photosynthesis.

84
Science Simulation Lab

Science Simulation Lab

Applying/Analyzing - "Science Simulation Lab"

Students use computer simulations to apply and analyze scientific concepts.

For example, students can use a simulation to model the behavior of atoms and molecules.

85

Science Debate Club

Science Debate Club

Analyzing/Evaluating - "Science Debate Club"

Students participate in debates on scientific topics, analyzing and evaluating evidence to support their arguments.

For example, students can debate the pros and cons of genetically modified organisms in agriculture.

86
Science Invention Competition

Science Invention Competition

Creating/Evaluating - "Science Invention Competition"

Students compete to develop the most innovative and effective scientific invention, using creativity and critical thinking to evaluate the strengths and weaknesses of different designs.

For example, students can compete to create a device that measures air pollution in their community.

87
Science Debate for Sustainable Development

Science for Sustainable Development

Linguistic Intelligence/Sustainable Development Goals - "Science Debate for Sustainable Development"

Students participate in debates on scientific topics related to sustainable development goals, developing their linguistic intelligence while learning about environmental sustainability.

For example, students can debate the use of renewable energy sources versus fossil fuels to meet energy needs.

88

Science Problem-Solving Challenge

Science Problem-Solving Challenge

Logical-Mathematical Intelligence/Sustainable Development Goals - "Science Problem-Solving Challenge"

Students solve real-world scientific problems related to sustainable development goals, using their logical-mathematical intelligence to develop innovative solutions.

For example, students can design a water filtration system for a community facing water scarcity.

89
Science Design Challenge

Science Design Challenge

Spatial Intelligence/Sustainable Development Goals - "Science Design Challenge"

Students use their spatial intelligence to design and create models of sustainable structures, such as energy-efficient buildings or greenhouses.

For example, students can design and build a model of a sustainable house that incorporates renewable energy and water conservation.

90

Science Songs for Sustainability

Science Songs for Sustainability

Musical Intelligence/Sustainable Development Goals - "Science Songs for Sustainability"

Students create and perform songs that raise awareness of sustainable development goals, using their musical intelligence to communicate scientific concepts.

For example, students can write and perform a song about the importance of biodiversity conservation.

91

Science Hands-On Lab

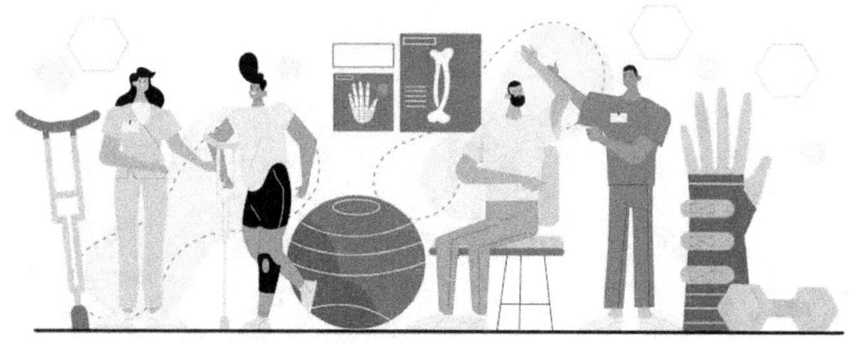

Science Hands-On Lab

Bodily-Kinesthetic Intelligence/Sustainable Development Goals - "Science Hands-On Lab"

Students participate in hands-on experiments related to sustainable development goals, using their bodily-kinesthetic intelligence to learn about scientific concepts through physical activity.

For example, students can build and test a simple solar cooker to learn about renewable energy.

92

Science Collaborative Projects

Science Collaborative Projects

Interpersonal Intelligence/Sustainable Development Goals - "Science Collaborative Projects"

Students work together in groups to research and develop projects related to sustainable development goals, using their interpersonal intelligence to communicate and collaborate effectively.

For example, students can develop a project to reduce plastic waste in their school or community.

93
Science Reflection Journals

Science Reflection Journals

Intrapersonal Intelligence/Sustainable Development Goals - "Science Reflection Journals"

Students use reflection journals to develop their intrapersonal intelligence, reflecting on their learning and experiences related to sustainable development goals.

For example, students can write reflections on the impacts of climate change on their community and their role in reducing greenhouse gas emissions.

94

Science Nature Exploration

Science Nature Exploration

Naturalist Intelligence/Sustainable Development Goals - "Science Nature Exploration"

Students explore the natural world and learn about the scientific principles that underpin sustainable development goals, using their naturalist intelligence to observe and analyze the environment.

For example, students can visit a local park or nature reserve to study the biodiversity of the area and learn about the importance of conservation.

95
Science Ethics and Values Discussions

Science Ethics and Values Discussions

Existential Intelligence/Sustainable Development Goals - "Science Ethics and Values Discussions"

Students engage in discussions and debates on the ethical and moral issues related to sustainable development goals, using their existential intelligence to reflect on the deeper meaning and purpose of their science learning.

For example, students can discuss the ethical considerations surrounding the use of genetically modified organisms in agriculture.

96

Science Project-Based Learning

Science Project-Based Learning

Multiple Intelligences/Sustainable Development Goals - "Science Project-Based Learning"

Students engage in project-based learning that incorporates multiple intelligences and addresses sustainable development goals, using their unique strengths and skills to develop innovative solutions to environmental challenges.

For example, students can work on a project to design and implement a recycling program in their school or community.

97
Collaborative Idea Generation

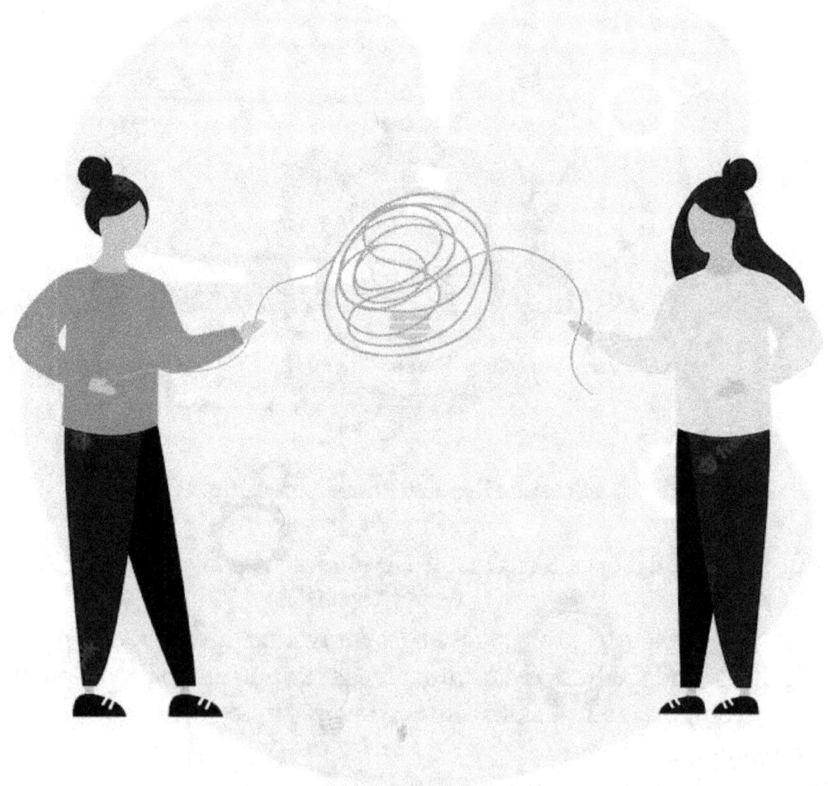

Collaborative Idea Generation

Think-Pair-Share - "Collaborative Idea Generation"

Explanation: Students think individually about a question or topic, pair up with a partner to discuss their ideas, and share their ideas with the whole class.

Example: What are some ways we can reduce our carbon footprint? Think about it on your own, pair up with a partner to discuss your ideas, and then share your ideas with the class.

98
Observation and Inquiry

Observation and Inquiry

See-Think-Wonder - "Observation and Inquiry"
Explanation: Students observe an object or image, share what they see, make connections, and ask questions to promote curiosity and inquiry.

Example: Look at this picture of a plant. What do you see? What do you think is happening in the picture? What questions do you have about the plant?

99

Metacognitive Reflection

Metacognitive Reflection

I Used to Think, But Now I Think - "Metacognitive Reflection"
Explanation: Students reflect on how their thinking has changed or evolved over time, encouraging metacognition and reflection on learning.

Example: I used to think that the Earth was flat, but now I think that it is round because I have learned about maps and globes.

100
Empathy and Perspective-Taking

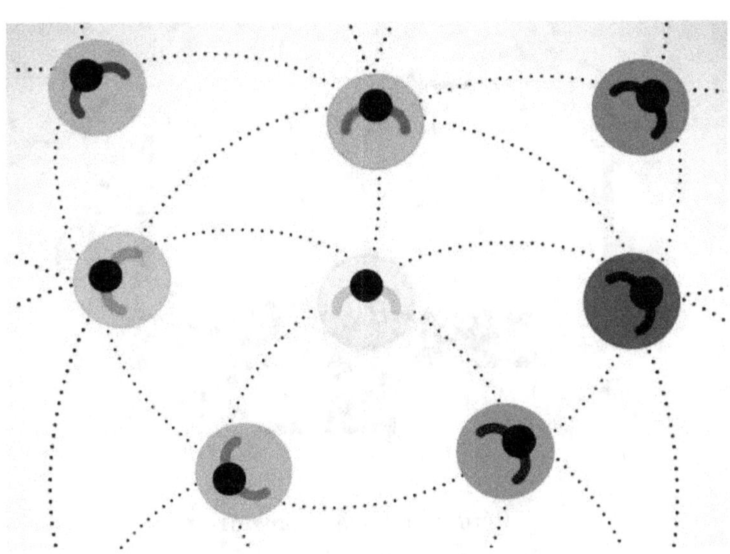

Empathy and Perspective-Taking

Circle of Viewpoints - "Empathy and Perspective-Taking"

Explanation: Students discuss a topic from multiple perspectives, developing empathy and understanding of diverse viewpoints.

Example: How might different animals view this environment? Imagine you are a bird, a rabbit, and a worm. What would each animal see and experience in this environment?

101

Evidence-Based Reasoning

Evidence-Based Reasoning

Claim-Support-Question - "Evidence-Based Reasoning"
Explanation: Students make a claim or argument, provide supporting evidence, and ask questions to deepen their understanding of the topic.

Example: What is the best way to keep our environment clean? Make a claim, provide evidence to support your claim, and ask questions to learn more about the topic.

102

Building on Prior Knowledge

Building on Prior Knowledge

Connect-Extend-Challenge - "Building on Prior Knowledge"
Explanation: Students make connections between new and prior knowledge, extend their understanding, and identify challenges or questions that arise.

Example: How is this plant similar to other plants we have learned about? How does it extend our understanding? What challenges or questions does it raise?

103
Visual Thinking

Visual Thinking

Color-Symbol-Image - "Visual Thinking"
Explanation: Students use colors, symbols, and images to represent their understanding of a topic, encouraging visual thinking and creativity.

Example: Use colors, symbols, and images to represent the parts of a plant and their functions.

104

Making Connections and Summarizing

Making Connections and Summarizing

3-2-1 Bridge - "Making Connections and Summarizing"

Explanation: Students identify three ideas they had before the lesson, two new ideas they learned, and one question they still have, connecting prior knowledge to new learning.

Example: What did you know about rocks before this lesson? What are two new things you learned? What is one question you still have about rocks?

105
Summarizing and Synthesizing

Summarizing and Synthesizing

Headlines - "Summarizing and Synthesizing"
Explanation: Students create a catchy headline or title that summarizes their understanding of a topic, synthesizing their learning.

Example: Create a headline that summarizes what you have learned about the water cycle.

106
Silent Brainstorming

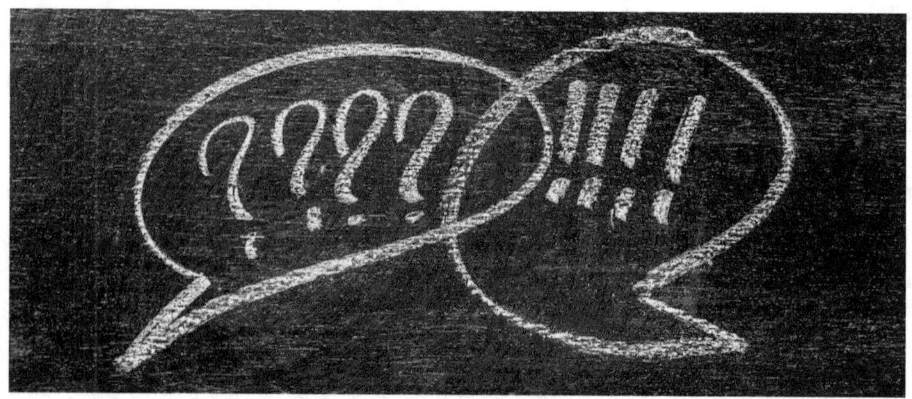

Silent Brainstorming

Chalk Talk - "Silent Brainstorming"
Explanation: Students brainstorm ideas or questions on a topic, silently writing and responding to each other's ideas on a shared chart or board.

Example: Brainstorm different ways that we can save water. Write your ideas on the chalkboard and respond to each other's ideas silently.

107
Empathy and Perspective-Taking

Empathy and Perspective-Taking

Step Inside - "Empathy and Perspective-Taking"

Explanation: Students imagine themselves as a character or object in a story or situation, developing empathy and understanding of diverse perspectives.

Example: Step inside the shoes of a tree during the changing seasons. What would the tree see, hear, and feel? How does it adapt to the changing environment?

108
Observation and Detail

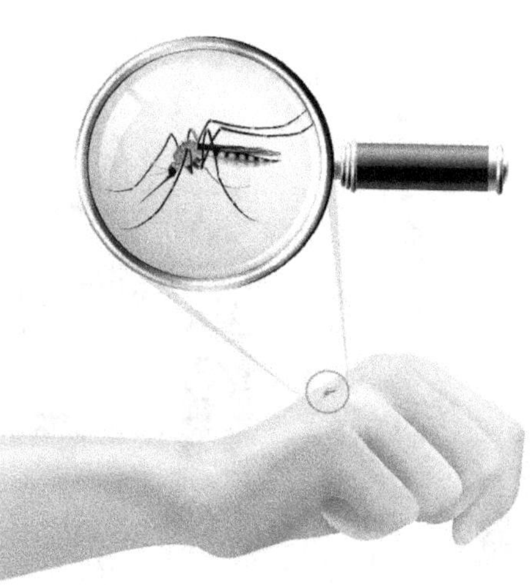

Observation and Detail

Zoom In - "Observation and Detail"

Explanation: Students observe a photograph or object, zoom in on details, and make inferences and connections.

Example: Zoom in on a rock. What details do you notice? What can you infer about the rock's formation and history?

109

Close Reading and Analysis

Close Reading and Analysis

Sentence-Phrase-Word - "Close Reading and Analysis"
Explanation: Students select a sentence, phrase, and word from a text or image, analyzing the meaning and significance of each.

Example: Select a sentence, phrase, and word from a science article. What do each of these selections tell us about the topic? Why are they important?

110

Evidence-Based Reasoning and Argumentation

Evidence-Based Reasoning and Argumentation

Claim-Evidence-Reasoning - "Evidence-Based Reasoning and Argumentation"

Explanation: Students make a claim or argument, provide supporting evidence, and explain their reasoning and thinking.

Example: Make a claim about the importance of biodiversity in an ecosystem. Provide evidence to support your claim and explain your reasoning.

111
Exploring Different Perspectives

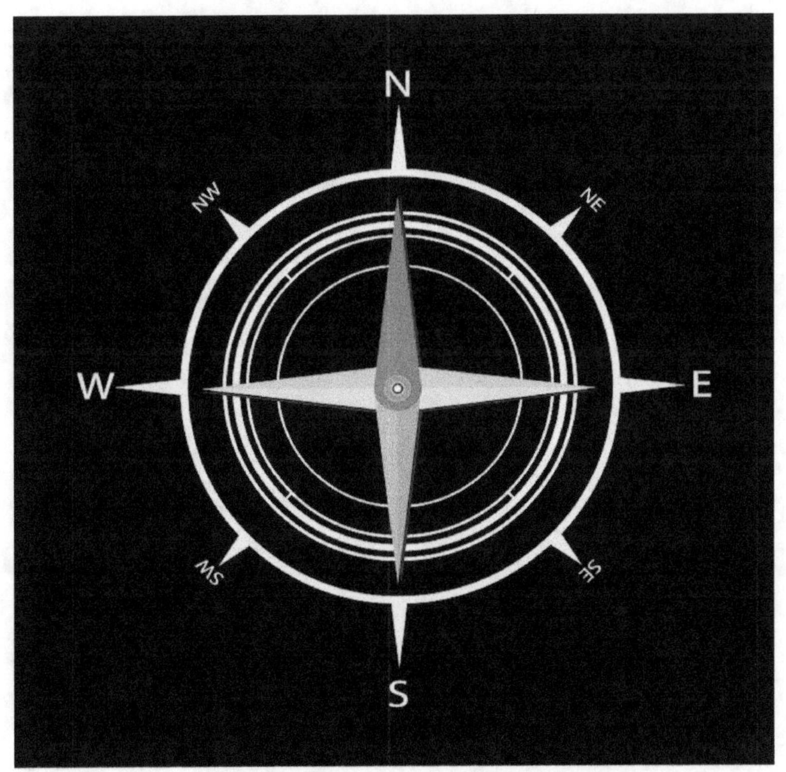

Exploring Different Perspectives

Compass Points - "Exploring Different Perspectives"

Explanation: Students explore different perspectives on a topic by discussing four key points: North (optimism), South (pessimism), East (new ideas), and West (caution).

Example: Discuss the impact of climate change on the environment from the four compass points. What are some optimistic, pessimistic, new, and cautious ideas about the topic?

112

Evidence-Based Reasoning and Explanation

Evidence-Based Reasoning and Explanation

What Makes You Say That? - "Evidence-Based Reasoning and Explanation"

Explanation: Students provide evidence and reasoning to support their observations, ideas, and interpretations.

Example: Why do you think this plant has such large leaves? What makes you say that? Provide evidence and reasoning to support your answer.

113
Vocabulary and Concept Development

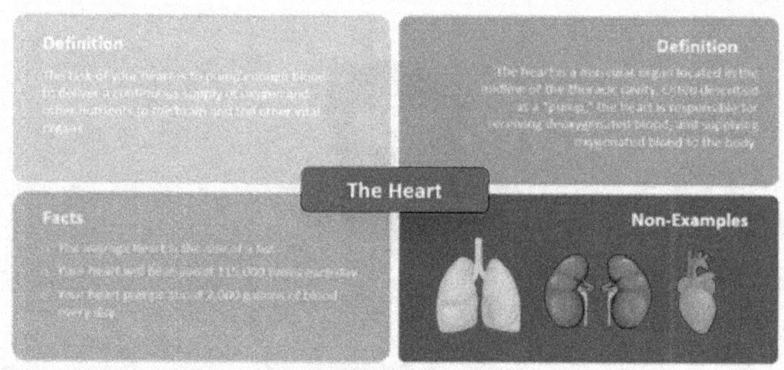

Vocabulary and Concept Developmen

Frayer Model - "Vocabulary and Concept Development"
Explanation: Students define a vocabulary word, provide examples and non-examples, and describe the characteristics and features of the word.

Example: Define the term "photosynthesis" using the Frayer Model. Provide examples and non-examples, and describe the characteristics and features of the term.

114

Critical Thinking and Problem-Solving

Critical Thinking and Problem-Solving

4C's - "Critical Thinking and Problem-Solving"

Explanation: Students use the 4C's (collaboration, communication, critical thinking, and creativity) to solve a real-world problem or challenge.

Example: Use the 4C's to design a sustainable garden that minimizes water use and maximizes biodiversity.

115

Change Over Time and Historical Thinking

Change Over Time and Historical Thinking

Headlines Across Time - "Change Over Time and Historical Thinking"

Explanation: Students create a headline that captures the essence of a scientific concept or idea at different points in history, identifying changes over time.

Example: Create a headline that captures the essence of the theory of evolution at different points in history. How has our understanding of evolution changed over time?

116
Persuasive Argumentation and Debate

Persuasive Argumentation and Debate

Tug-of-War - "Persuasive Argumentation and Debate"

Explanation: Students argue for or against a scientific concept or idea, providing evidence and reasoning to support their arguments.

Example: Should humans use genetically modified organisms (GMOs) in food production? Divide into two teams and have a tug-of-war debate, arguing for or against the use of GMOs.

117

Understanding Different Perspectives

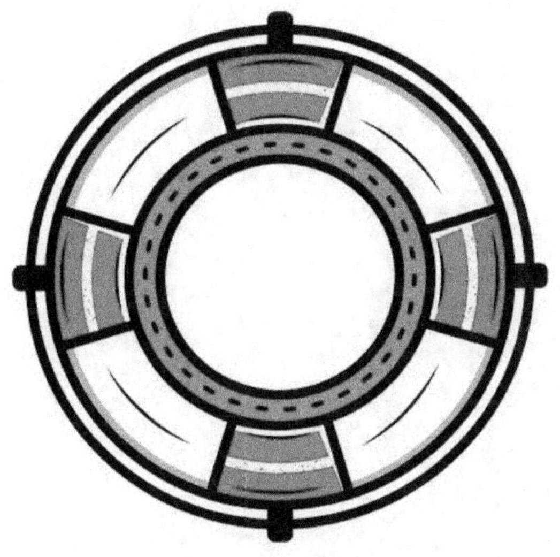

Understanding Different Perspectives

Circle of Viewpoints - "Understanding Different Perspectives"
Explanation: Students identify and explore different viewpoints related to a topic, understanding how different people may see the same thing in different ways.

Example: Explore different viewpoints related to the impact of pollution on the environment. How might different people (such as scientists, business owners, and community members) see this issue differently?

118
Understanding Systems and Relationships

Parts Purpose Complexities

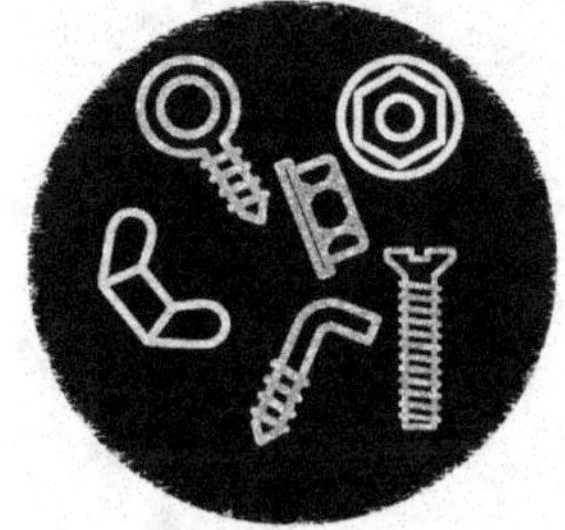  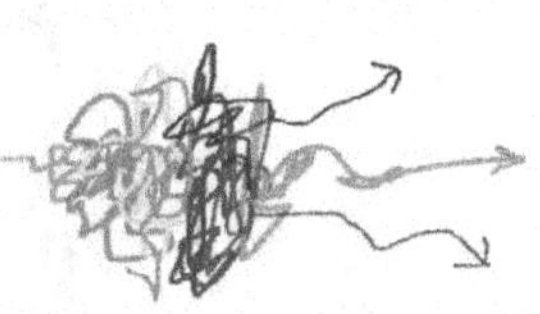

Understanding Systems and Relationships

Parts, Purposes, Complexities - "Understanding Systems and Relationships"

Explanation: Students break down a system or object into its parts, identifying their purposes and complexities, and analyzing how they work together.

Example: Analyze the parts, purposes, and complexities of a solar panel system. How do the different parts work together to generate electricity from sunlight?

119

Building Connections and Expanding Thinking

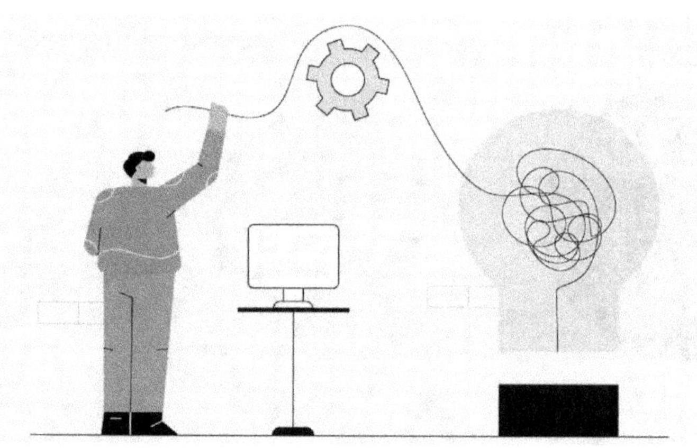

Building Connections and Expanding Thinking

Connect-Extend-Challenge - "Building Connections and Expanding Thinking"

Explanation: Students make connections between new information and their prior knowledge, extend their thinking based on new insights, and challenge themselves to ask new questions and explore further.

Example: Connect new information about the water cycle to what you already know. How does this information extend your thinking about how water moves through the environment? What questions do you now have?

120
Observation and Inquiry

Observation and Inquiry

See-Think-Wonder - "Observation and Inquiry"

Explanation: Students make observations about an object or image, share their initial thoughts and interpretations, and generate questions to guide further inquiry.

Example: Observe an animal in its natural habitat. What do you see? What might this animal be thinking or feeling? What questions do you have about this animal and its environment?

121
Summarizing and Synthesizing Information

Summarizing and Synthesizing Information

Headlines - "Summarizing and Synthesizing Information"

Explanation: Students summarize key information about a topic in a headline format, synthesizing information from multiple sources and perspectives.

Example: Write a headline summarizing the key ideas about the causes and effects of climate change. How can you synthesize information from different sources to create a clear and concise summary?

122

Asking Effective Questions

Asking Effective Questions

Question Starts - "Asking Effective Questions"

Explanation: Students practice asking effective questions that promote curiosity, inquiry, and a deeper understanding of a topic.

Example: Generate a list of question starts that could be used to explore the life cycle of a butterfly. How can you ask questions that promote deeper understanding of this process?

123
Collaborative Thinking and Sharing

Collaborative Thinking and Sharing

Think-Pair-Share - "Collaborative Thinking and Sharing"
Explanation: Students think about a question or problem individually, pair up with a partner to share their ideas and insights, and then share with

the larger group.

Example: Use think-pair-share to explore the question "How do living things adapt to their environments?" What ideas and insights can you gain from working collaboratively with your peers?

124
Reflecting and Revising Thinking

Reflecting and Revising Thinking

I Used to Think...Now I Think... - "Reflecting and Revising Thinking" Explanation: Students reflect on their prior knowledge and assumptions about a topic, share how their thinking has changed based on new information and insights, and revise their understanding accordingly.

Example: Use the "I used to think...now I think..." routine to reflect on how your understanding of the solar system has evolved over time. How have new discoveries and insights changed your thinking?

125

Generating and Sharing Ideas

Generating and Sharing Ideas

Chalk Talk - "Generating and Sharing Ideas"
Explanation: Students generate ideas and insights related to a topic, writing them down on a shared surface (such as a chalkboard or large piece of paper), and then discussing and analyzing the ideas together.

Example: Use chalk talk to generate and share ideas related to the importance of biodiversity in an ecosystem. How can you use this collaborative process to gain new insights and perspectives?

126
Reflecting on Learning and Growth

Reflecting on Learning and Growth

Circle of Reflection - "Reflecting on Learning and Growth"
Explanation: Students reflect on their learning and growth, sharing their insights and reflections with their peers, and identifying areas for further growth and development.

Example: Use the circle of reflection to reflect on what you have learned about the scientific method. How have you grown and developed as a scientist? What areas do you still need to work on to continue growing and improving?

127

Plant a Seed, Watch it Grow: Discover the Wonders of Plant Life!

Plant a Sapling, Plant Happiness

"Plants are essential to life on Earth, providing us with the air we breathe and the food we eat. Discover the wonders of plant life by learning about their different parts and functions, and by planting your own seeds and watching them grow. By understanding the importance of plants, we can learn to appreciate and protect the natural world around us."

"Discover the Wonders of Flowering Plants Through Art-Integrated Learning!"

Flower Power: Have students create a collage of the different parts of a flowering plant using different materials such as construction paper, tissue paper, and stickers.

❦❦❦

Petal Pals: Students can make their own paper flowers and label the different parts of the flower including the petals, stamen, and pistil.

❦❦❦

Rooted in Knowledge: Students can explore the different types of roots in a flowering plant by creating a 3D model using playdough or clay.

❦❦❦

Stem-tastic: Students can create their own stem structures using straws and pipe cleaners to learn about the different parts of a stem such as nodes, internodes, and buds.

❦❦❦

Pollinator Party: Students can learn about the importance of pollinators by creating their own paper bees and butterflies and exploring how they interact with the different parts of a flowering plant.

❦❦❦

Seed Sense: Students can learn about the different types of seeds and how they are dispersed by creating their own seed models using different materials such as beads and sequins.

❦❦❦

Fruit Frenzy: Students can learn about the different types of fruits in a flowering plant by creating their own fruit sculptures using clay or playdough.

❦❦❦

Photosynthesis Fun: Students can learn about the role of leaves in photosynthesis by creating their own leaf prints using paint and paper.

❦❦❦

Germination Celebration: Students can learn about the process of germination by creating their own mini gardens using soil and seedlings.

❦❦❦

Bloom Boom: Students can create their own flower garden by drawing and coloring different types of flowers and labeling the different parts of the flower.

❦❦❦

Plant Parenthood: Students can learn about reproduction in flowering plants by creating their own seed pods using clay and labeling the different parts of the flower involved in pollination and seed formation.

❦❦❦

Growing Up Green: Students can create their own 3D models of plant growth stages using recycled materials such as egg cartons, cardboard, and paint.

❦❦❦

Pollination Party: Students can learn about the role of pollinators in plant reproduction by creating their own paper bees and butterflies and exploring how they interact with different flowers.

❦❦❦

Life Cycle Lingo: Students can create a visual representation of the life cycle of a flowering plant by drawing and labeling the different stages of plant growth, from seed to adult plant.

❦❦❦

Green Thumb Fun: Students can learn about the different factors that affect plant growth by conducting their own experiments with different soil types, sunlight exposure, and watering techniques.

❧❧❧

Flower Powerhouse: Students can learn about the importance of photosynthesis in plant growth by creating their own 3D models of the different parts of a leaf and exploring how they work together to produce food for the plant.

❧❧❧

Garden Gurus: Students can design and create their own garden plot, including choosing which flowering plants to grow, how to care for them, and how to harvest their own vegetables and fruits.

❧❧❧

Rooted in Science: Students can learn about the different types of roots in a plant and how they help to anchor the plant and absorb nutrients by creating their own root systems using clay and other materials.

❧❧❧

Bloom Buddies: Students can learn about the different parts of a flower and how they work together to reproduce by creating their own paper flower models and labeling the different parts.

❧❧❧

Growing Greatness: Students can create their own growth charts to track the growth of their plants over time while learning about the importance of patience and perseverance in the process.

❧❧❧

"Step into the Fascinating World of Plant Habitats Through Art, Science, and Exploration!"

Habitat Heroes: Students can create their own dioramas of different plant habitats such as rainforests, deserts, and wetlands while learning about the different types of plants and animals that live in each environment.

❧❧❧

Botanical Bonanza: Students can learn about the different types of plants that grow in their local environment by going on a nature walk, collecting samples, and creating their own herbarium.

ϸϸϸ

Eco-Art Attack: Students can use recycled materials to create their own 3D models of different plant habitats, such as building a rainforest out of paper mache and cardboard.

ϸϸϸ

Nature's Palette: Students can explore the colors and patterns found in different plant habitats by creating their own nature-inspired art using materials such as leaves, flowers, and seeds.

ϸϸϸ

Garden Adventure: Students can create their own garden plots while learning about the different types of plants that grow best in different types of soil, sunlight, and moisture.

ϸϸϸ

Plant Explorer: Students can go on a scavenger hunt in their local environment while learning about the different types of plants and animals that live in each habitat.

ϸϸϸ

Botanical Blueprint: Students can learn about the different parts of a plant and how they help the plant to survive in different habitats, by creating their own 3D models of a plant using recycled materials.

ϸϸϸ

Earth's Garden: Students can learn about the importance of biodiversity and conservation by creating their own artwork inspired by the different plant habitats found around the world.

ϸϸϸ

Wild About Plants: Students can learn about the different types of plants that grow in different habitats by creating their own flipbook with illustrations and information about each plant.

ᏈᏈᏈ

Green Thumb Gazette: Students can create their own newspaper or magazine while learning about different plant habitats around the world, and the different ways in which humans impact these habitats.

ᏈᏈᏈ

128

From Furry Friends to Fierce Predators: Explore the Diversity of Animal Life!

From Furry Friends to Fierce Predators

"Animals come in all shapes and sizes, from tiny insects to enormous elephants, and each has its own unique features and behaviors. Explore the diversity of animal life by learning about different habitats, diets, and adaptations that help them survive in their environments. By understanding the importance of animal life, we can learn to appreciate and protect the natural world around us and the incredible creatures that inhabit it."

"Discover the Amazing World of Animal Lifestyles and Habitats Through Art, Science, and Exploration!"

Animal Kingdom Chronicles: Students can create their own illustrated storybooks while learning about the different lifestyles and habitats of animals around the world.

ᐅᐅᐅ

Creature Feature: Students can create their own 3D models of different animals while learning about the adaptations that allow them to thrive in their unique environments.

ᐅᐅᐅ

Eco-Explorers: Students can go on a nature walk and create their own animal observation journals while learning about the different behaviors and lifestyles of animals in their local environment.

ᐅᐅᐅ

Wildlife Wonders: Students can create their own nature-inspired art using materials such as feathers, leaves, and twigs, while learning about the different lifestyles and habitats of animals.

ᐅᐅᐅ

Animal Architects: Students can create their own 3D models of different animal habitats such as beaver dams and bird nests, while learning about the different materials and strategies used by animals to build their homes.

ᐅᐅᐅ

Habitat Heroes: Students can learn about the different types of animal habitats around the world while creating their own dioramas and artwork inspired by the animals that live in each environment.

ᐅᐅᐅ

Wild About Science: Students can conduct their own experiments and investigations while learning about the different adaptations and lifestyles of animals in different environments.

❧❧❧

Zoology Zone: Students can create their own animal identification guides while learning about the different physical and behavioral characteristics that distinguish different species.

❧❧❧

Animal Artifacts: Students can create their own art inspired by the different types of animal lifestyles, such as creating animal masks or sculptures using recycled materials.

❧❧❧

Nature Detectives: Students can go on a scavenger hunt and collect animal tracks, feathers, and other artifacts while learning about the different lifestyles and habitats of animals in their local environment.

❧❧❧

Join the Amazing World of Animal Reproduction Through Art, Science, and Exploration!"
   Animal Life Cycles: Students can create their own illustrated diagrams or flipbooks, while learning about the different stages of reproduction and life cycles of animals.

❧❧❧

Amazing Animal Offspring: Students can create their own artwork or models of animal babies, while learning about the different types of reproduction and development in animals.

❧❧❧

Nature's Miracle: Students can learn about the process of birth in animals, while creating their own art inspired by different animals giving birth, such as drawing or painting animal birth scenes.

❧❧❧

Animal Mating Dances: Students can create their own dance routines inspired by the mating rituals of different animals, while learning about the different ways in which animals attract and mate with their partners.

🐾🐾🐾

Life Bringers: Students can create their own art inspired by the different types of animal reproduction, such as drawing or painting animal parents caring for their young.

🐾🐾🐾

Egg-citing Adventures: Students can learn about the different types of eggs laid by different animals, while creating their own art or models of animal eggs.

🐾🐾🐾

Animal Matchmakers: Students can learn about the different ways in which animals find their mates, while creating their own art inspired by different animal courtship rituals.

🐾🐾🐾

Baby Animal Bonanza: Students can create their own baby animal identification guides, while learning about the different types of offspring produced by different animals.

🐾🐾🐾

Animal Family Trees: Students can create their own illustrated family trees for different types of animals, while learning about the different types of family structures and relationships found in the animal kingdom.

🐾🐾🐾

Animal Reproduction Olympics: Students can create their own games and challenges inspired by the different types of animal reproduction, such as racing to find hidden eggs or performing mating dances.

🐾🐾🐾

129

Healthy Habits for a Happy Body: Exploring the Wonders of Human Health and Hygiene!

Healthy Habits for a Happy Body

"Our bodies are amazing machines that require proper care to function at their best. By learning about the different systems and functions of the human body, as well as the importance of good hygiene and healthy habits, we can promote overall wellness and prevent illness. From washing our hands to staying active and eating nutritious foods, there are many ways to maintain a happy, healthy body. Join us on a journey to explore the wonders of human health and hygiene!"

"Discover the Amazing World of Bones, Joints, and Muscles Through Art, Science, and Movement!"

Skeletal System Superstars: Students can create their own 3D models of bones, while learning about the different types and functions of bones in the human body.

⫸⫸⫸

Muscle Makers: Students can create their own illustrated diagrams or flipbooks, while learning about the different types of muscles and how they work together to create movement.

⫸⫸⫸

Joint Jamboree: Students can create their own joint models, while learning about the different types and functions of joints in the human body.

⫸⫸⫸

Human Body Olympics: Students can create their own games and challenges inspired by the different parts of the human body, such as races that test the strength of muscles or flexibility of joints.

⫸⫸⫸

Bone Builders: Students can learn about the different types of nutrients needed for healthy bones, while creating their own art inspired by the food sources that provide these nutrients.

⫸⫸⫸

Dance Anatomy: Students can create their own dance routines inspired by the movements of different muscles and joints in the body, while learning about the different types of dance and how they relate to anatomy.

⫸⫸⫸

Muscle Memory Masters: Students can create their own memory games or flashcards, while learning about the different names and locations of muscles in the body.

ᐅᐅᐅ

Skeleton Scavenger Hunt: Students can go on a scavenger hunt to find bones in the environment, while learning about the different types and functions of bones in the human body.

ᐅᐅᐅ

Human Body Art: Students can create their own art inspired by the different parts of the human body, such as creating bone collages or muscle drawings.

ᐅᐅᐅ

Body Builders: Students can create their own workout routines inspired by the different parts of the human body, such as doing exercises that strengthen bones or muscles.

ᐅᐅᐅ

"Explore the Fascinating World of the Nervous System and Sense Organs Through Art, Science, and Sensory Adventures!"
    Brain Builders: Students can create their own illustrated diagrams or models of the brain, while learning about the different parts and functions of the nervous system.

ᐅᐅᐅ

Senses Safari: Students can go on a sensory scavenger hunt to explore the world around them, while learning about the different sense organs and how they work.

ᐅᐅᐅ

Nervous System Olympics: Students can create their own games and challenges inspired by the different parts of the nervous system, such as testing reflexes or memory.

ᐅᐅᐅ

Mind Maps: Students can create their own mind maps to explore the different connections between the brain and the sense organs, while learning about how they work together to process information.

ᐅᐅᐅ

Sense-tational Art: Students can create their own art inspired by the different senses, such as painting with different textures or creating music with everyday objects.

❦❦❦

Brain Boosters: Students can learn about the different ways to keep their brains healthy, while creating their own art inspired by brain-boosting activities like exercise or reading.

❦❦❦

Sensory Storytelling: Students can create their own stories or comics inspired by the different senses, while learning about how the brain processes information and creates meaning.

❦❦❦

Sensory Snacks: Students can explore the different tastes and textures of food, while learning about how the sense of taste works and how it's connected to the brain.

❦❦❦

Brain Busters: Students can create their own brain teasers or puzzles, while learning about how the brain processes information and solves problems.

❦❦❦

Nervous System Nature Walk: Students can take a nature walk and observe the different sensory experiences, while learning about the different sense organs and how they work.

❦❦❦

"Discover the Exciting World of Food, Health, and Safety Through Art, Science, and Fun!"

Healthy Plate Art: Students can create their own art inspired by the different food groups and how to make a healthy plate, while learning about the importance of balanced nutrition.

❦❦❦

Food Detectives: Students can go on a food scavenger hunt to learn about the different types of foods and where they come from, while learning about the importance of eating a variety of foods.

ƥƥƥ

Cooking Challenge: Students can create their own healthy recipes, while learning about the different types of food and how to prepare them safely.

ƥƥƥ

Food Safety Superheroes: Students can learn about the different ways to keep food safe and prevent foodborne illness, while creating their own art inspired by food safety practices.

ƥƥƥ

My Body My Choice: Students can create their own health journals or fitness plans, while learning about the importance of exercise and self-care for a healthy body and mind.

ƥƥƥ

Food Artisans: Students can learn about the different jobs and skills involved in producing and preparing food, while creating their own art inspired by the world of food.

ƥƥƥ

Nutrition Ninjas: Students can create their own superhero characters or comic strips, while learning about the different types of nutrients and their importance for a healthy body.

ƥƥƥ

Mindful Eating: Students can practice mindful eating techniques, while learning about the importance of being present and mindful during meal times.

ƥƥƥ

Safety Stars: Students can learn about the different safety hazards in the kitchen and how to prevent accidents, while creating their own safety posters or videos.

ƥƥƥ

Food Fun and Fitness: Students can create their own games and challenges inspired by healthy eating and fitness, while learning about the importance of staying active and making healthy choices.

ᐯᐯᐯ

130
Rock Your World: Discovering the Magic of Rocks, Salts, and Minerals!

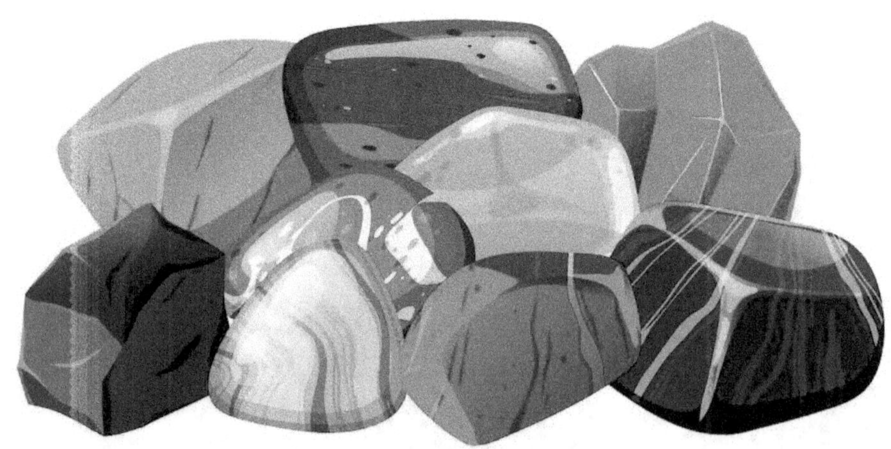

Rock Your World

"Rocks, salts, and minerals may seem like ordinary objects, but they are actually incredibly fascinating and important to our everyday lives. From the colorful crystals of a salt rock lamp to the sparkling gems of a mineral collection, there is so much to discover about these natural wonders. Learn about the different types of rocks, how they are formed, and how they are used in everyday objects. Explore the unique properties of salts and minerals, from healing properties to industrial applications. Join us on a journey to rock your world by discovering the magic of rocks, salts, and minerals!"

"Get Rockin' and Rollin' with the Exciting World of Rocks and Minerals Through Art, Science, and Adventure!"

Rock and Roll Art: Students can create their own rock-inspired art pieces, while learning about the different types of rocks and how they're formed.

ᐅᐅᐅ

Mineral Detectives: Students can go on a mineral scavenger hunt to learn about the different types of minerals and where they can be found, while learning about their properties.

ᐅᐅᐅ

Rock Collectors: Students can start their own rock collections and learn about the different types of rocks and minerals, while practicing their observation and classification skills.

ᐅᐅᐅ

Gemstone Treasures: Students can learn about the different types of precious and semi-precious gemstones, while creating their own jewelry or art inspired by the beauty of these minerals.

ᐅᐅᐅ

Rock Cycle Adventures: Students can create their own illustrated stories or models of the rock cycle, while learning about the different stages and processes involved in the formation of rocks.

ᐅᐅᐅ

Crystal Creators: Students can create their own crystal formations using household materials, while learning about the different types of crystals and how they're formed.

ᐅᐅᐅ

Fossil Hunters: Students can learn about the different types of fossils and how they provide evidence of past life on Earth, while creating their own fossil replicas or illustrations.

꧂꧂꧂

Rock Star Science: Students can create their own experiments and investigations to explore the properties of different types of rocks and minerals, while learning about the scientific method.

꧂꧂꧂

Earth Explorers: Students can learn about the different layers of the Earth and the role that rocks and minerals play in shaping our planet, while creating their own art inspired by Earth's natural wonders.

꧂꧂꧂

Mineral Madness: Students can create their own games and challenges inspired by the different types of minerals and their properties, while practicing their critical thinking and problem-solving skills.

꧂꧂꧂

"Join the Soil Conservation Squad and Explore the Exciting World of Soil Erosion and Conservation Through Art, Science, and Action!"

Soil Artifacts: Students can create their own art pieces inspired by soil samples, while learning about the different layers of soil and their importance for plant growth.

꧂꧂꧂

Erosion Explorers: Students can create their own experiments and investigations to explore the causes and effects of soil erosion, while learning about the importance of soil conservation.

꧂꧂꧂

Soil Superheroes: Students can create their own superhero characters or comic strips, while learning about the different ways to prevent soil erosion and promote soil health.

꧂꧂꧂

Dirt Detectives: Students can go on a soil scavenger hunt to learn about the different types of soil and their properties, while learning about the importance of soil conservation.

꧂꧂꧂

Garden Gurus: Students can create their own mini gardens or terrariums, while learning about the different ways to conserve soil and promote plant growth.

🍂🍂🍂

Nature Navigators: Students can go on a nature walk to observe different types of soil and their surroundings, while learning about the importance of soil conservation for ecosystems.

🍂🍂🍂

Earth Artists: Students can create their own art pieces inspired by the beauty of natural landscapes, while learning about the importance of soil conservation for preserving our planet's natural resources.

🍂🍂🍂

Soil Science Sleuths: Students can conduct soil tests to learn about the different properties of soil and how they impact plant growth, while learning about the importance of soil conservation.

🍂🍂🍂

Erosion Busters: Students can create their own inventions or designs to prevent soil erosion, while learning about the engineering process and the importance of problem-solving skills.

🍂🍂🍂

Soil Stewards: Students can create their own pledges or action plans to conserve soil in their own communities, while learning about the importance of taking action to protect our environment.

🍂🍂🍂

131

Breath of Life: Exploring the Vital Importance of Air and Water to Our Planet!

Breath of Life

"Air and water are two of the most essential elements to life on Earth, supporting everything from plants to animals to humans. However, they are also fragile resources that require careful attention and conservation. Join us on a journey to explore the vital importance of air and water, from the science of the water cycle to the composition of our atmosphere. Learn about the different ways we use and impact these resources, and discover how we can all play a role in protecting them for generations to come. Let's celebrate the breath of life that air and water provide!"

"Dive into the World of Air and Water Conservation through Art, Science, and Action and Become a Guardian of our Planet's Natural Resources!"

Air and Water Art: Students can create their own art pieces inspired by the beauty of air and water, while learning about the importance of these natural resources for life on Earth.

ᵽᵽᵽ

Pollution Patrol: Students can create their own games or challenges to learn about the different types of air and water pollution and their effects on the environment and human health.

ᵽᵽᵽ

Water Wise: Students can create their own water conservation posters or slogans, while learning about the importance of water conservation and the ways they can save water in their daily lives.

ᵽᵽᵽ

Weather Watchers: Students can create their own weather reports or illustrations, while learning about the different types of weather patterns and the role of air in shaping our climate.

ᵽᵽᵽ

Air and Water Adventurers: Students can go on a nature walk or field trip to observe the different types of air and water environments, while learning about the importance of environmental conservation.

ᵽᵽᵽ

Aqua Artists: Students can create their own watercolor paintings inspired by different water environments and creatures, while learning about the importance of protecting our water resources.

ᵽᵽᵽ

Air Science Explorers: Students can conduct their own experiments or investigations to learn about the properties of air and how they impact our daily lives, while learning about the scientific method.

ᐳᐳᐳ

Water Guardians: Students can create their own water filtration systems or designs to clean up polluted water, while learning about the importance of protecting our water resources.

ᐳᐳᐳ

Nature Detectives: Students can go on a scavenger hunt to learn about the different types of air and water creatures and their habitats, while learning about the importance of biodiversity and environmental conservation.

ᐳᐳᐳ

Air and Water Action Heroes: Students can create their own action plans or pledges to protect our air and water resources, while learning about the importance of taking action to protect our environment.

ᐳᐳᐳ

132

Power Up: Discovering the Wonders of Force, Work, and Energy!

Power Up: Discovering the Wonders of Force, Work, and Energy

"Force, work, and energy are all around us, driving everything from the movement of objects to the sounds we hear. Join us on a journey to explore the power of these fundamental concepts, from the physics of motion to the chemistry of combustion. Learn about the different types of energy, how they are transformed and harnessed, and the impact they have on our daily lives. Discover how we can all use these forces for good, whether it's through sustainable energy sources or inventions that make our lives easier. Let's power up and unlock the wonders of force, work, and energy!"

"Join the Energy Adventure and Discover the Exciting World of Force, Work, and Energy through Art, Science, and Action!"

Energy Explorers: Students can create their own experiments or investigations to learn about the different forms of energy and how they can be transformed, while learning about the scientific method.

ᛈᛈᛈ

Work Wizards: Students can create their own machines or devices to make work easier, while learning about the principles of force, work, and energy.

ᛈᛈᛈ

Kinetic Creations: Students can create their own kinetic art pieces or sculptures, while learning about the relationship between motion and energy.

ᛈᛈᛈ

Energy Efficient: Students can create their own energy conservation posters or slogans, while learning about the importance of conserving energy and the ways they can save energy in their daily lives.

ᛈᛈᛈ

Forces of Nature: Students can create their own illustrations or models to represent different types of natural forces, such as wind, water, or gravity, while learning about the principles of force and energy.

ᛈᛈᛈ

Mechanical Marvels: Students can create their own mechanical toys or contraptions, while learning about the principles of force, work, and energy.

ᛈᛈᛈ

Energy Detectives: Students can go on a scavenger hunt to find different sources of energy and learn about their properties and uses, while learning about the importance of energy conservation.

ᛈᛈᛈ

Power Painters: Students can create their own paintings or murals inspired by different sources of energy, such as the sun or wind, while learning about the importance of renewable energy sources.

ᛏᛏᛏ

Energy Heroes: Students can create their own action plans or pledges to conserve energy and reduce their carbon footprint, while learning about the importance of taking action to protect our planet.

ᛏᛏᛏ

Electric Explorers: Students can create their own electric circuits or devices, while learning about the principles of electricity and energy.

ᛏᛏᛏ

"Get Ready to Invent, Experiment, and Explore the Amazing World of Simple Machines with Art and Science!"

Rube Goldberg Machines: Students can create their own Rube Goldberg machines using simple machines, while learning about the principles of force, work, and energy.

ᛏᛏᛏ

Simple Machines Olympics: Students can participate in a simple machines olympics where they compete in different events that showcase the power and efficiency of simple machines.

ᛏᛏᛏ

Inventor's Workshop: Students can create their own inventions using simple machines, while learning about the creative process and the importance of innovation.

ᛏᛏᛏ

Simple Machines Scavenger Hunt: Students can go on a scavenger hunt to find different examples of simple machines in their everyday lives, while learning about the different types of simple machines and their uses.

ᛏᛏᛏ

Pulley Power: Students can create their own pulley systems and experiment with different weights and distances, while learning about the principles of force and work.

❧❧❧

Lever Lab: Students can experiment with different types of levers and see how they can be used to lift heavy objects with ease, while learning about the principles of force and energy.

❧❧❧

Wheel and Axle Adventures: Students can create their own vehicles or machines using the wheel and axle, while learning about the importance of this simple machine in our daily lives.

❧❧❧

Inclined Plane Party: Students can create their own ramps and explore how they can be used to move objects from one place to another, while learning about the principles of force and work.

❧❧❧

Screw Science: Students can create their own screws and experiment with different shapes and sizes, while learning about the principles of force and energy.

❧❧❧

Gears Galore: Students can create their own gear systems and explore how they can be used to transfer power and motion, while learning about the principles of force, work, and energy.

❧❧❧

133

Beyond the Horizon: Discovering the Wonders of Heavenly Bodies, Space, and the Universe!

Beyond the Horizon

"The universe is vast and mysterious, full of incredible objects and phenomena that stretch beyond our wildest imagination. From the stars and planets of our solar system to the black holes and galaxies of the cosmos, there is so much to explore and discover. Join us on a journey to uncover the wonders of heavenly bodies, space, and the universe, from the science of astronomy to the history of space exploration. Learn about the different types of telescopes, space missions, and scientific discoveries that have expanded our understanding of the universe. Let's journey beyond the horizon and unlock the secrets of the cosmos!"

"Discovering the Wonders of Heavenly Bodies, Space, and the Universe"

Moon Craters Art Project: Students can create their own moon craters using different materials, while learning about the moon's surface and how craters are formed.

𐤐𐤐𐤐

Solar System Mobile: Students can create their own solar system mobiles using different materials and colors, while learning about the planets and their orbits.

𐤐𐤐𐤐

Sun Prints: "Let the Sun do the Artwork"

Collect different shapes of leaves, flowers, and objects, place them on sun-sensitive paper and let the Sun create a beautiful print.

𐤐𐤐𐤐

Moon Phase Collage: "Let's explore the Moon's different faces"

Cut out different shapes of the Moon from black construction paper and let students arrange them in the correct sequence of phases.

𐤐𐤐𐤐

Constellation Creation: "Discover the beauty of the night sky"

Have students create their own constellations by connecting stars with a white pencil on black paper, and then use glitter glue to highlight the stars.

𐤐𐤐𐤐

Planet Models: "Create your own Universe"

Use papier-mache to make planet models of different sizes and colors, and then have students paint and label them accordingly.

𐤐𐤐𐤐

Galaxy Art: "Let's make a space masterpiece"

Use black paper, white chalk, and colored chalk to create a galaxy-themed artwork with stars, planets, and nebulas.

ᐳᐳᐳ

Rocket Launch: "Blast off to Space!"

Have students make their own paper rockets and launch them outside, measuring how far they go and exploring the concepts of thrust and trajectory.

ᐳᐳᐳ

Space Suit Design: "Design your own Space Suit"

Have students create their own space suits using recycled materials, considering the challenges of living and working in space.

ᐳᐳᐳ

Planet Travel Brochure: "Plan your Space Vacation"

Have students research different planets and create a travel brochure advertising the unique features of each planet.

ᐳᐳᐳ

Sun and Moon Dance: "Let's dance with the Heavenly Bodies"

Have students create a dance routine that depicts the movements and interactions of the Sun and Moon, exploring concepts of day and night, seasons, and eclipses.

ᐳᐳᐳ

Starry Night Sky: "Create a Starry Night inside the Classroom"

Have students create their own version of Van Gogh's "Starry Night" by painting a night sky scene with different colors and shapes of stars, planets, and the Moon.

ᐳᐳᐳ

Space Rocket Art: "Blast Off to New Frontiers"

Have students use construction paper and paint to create their own rocket ships and launch them into space.

ᐳᐳᐳ

Solar System Model: "Discover the Planets in our Solar System"

Have students use papier-mache to create a model of the solar system and paint the planets in different colors.

ᐅᐅᐅ

Moon Crater Art: "Explore the Surface of the Moon"
Have students create a painting or drawing of the Moon's surface, including craters and other interesting features.

ᐅᐅᐅ

Space Food Art: "Design your own Space Meal"
Have students design and draw their own space meals, considering the challenges of preparing food in zero gravity.

ᐅᐅᐅ

Starry Night Sky Art: "Experience the Wonders of Space"
Have students use glitter and paint to create a starry night sky artwork, including constellations and shooting stars.

ᐅᐅᐅ

Alien Drawing: "Create your own Extraterrestrial Life"
Have students create a drawing or painting of an alien that they think could exist on another planet.

ᐅᐅᐅ

Space Suit Design: "Create a Suit for your Space Adventure"
Have students design and draw their own space suits, considering the challenges of living and working in space.

ᐅᐅᐅ

Moon Landing Collage: "Celebrate the First Lunar Landing"
Have students create a collage that commemorates the first lunar landing, using newspaper clippings, photographs, and other materials.

ᐅᐅᐅ

Mars Rover Art: "Explore the Red Planet"
Have students create a painting or drawing of a Mars rover exploring the planet's surface.

ᐅᐅᐅ

Space Station Model: "Build a Model of a Space Station"

Have students use recycled materials to create a model of a space station, considering the challenges of living and working in space.

ᐁᐁᐁ

Remember to adapt the activities according to the age and interests of your students, and have fun exploring the mysteries of space!

134

Protecting Our Home: Discovering the Importance of Saving and Preserving Our Environment!

Protecting Our Home

"Our environment is a precious resource that provides us with the air we breathe, the water we drink, and the food we eat. However, it is also under threat from pollution, climate change, and other human activities. Join us on a journey to explore the importance of saving and preserving our environment, from the impact of deforestation on wildlife to the effects of plastic waste on our oceans. Learn about the different ways we can all make a difference, whether it's through reducing our carbon footprint, supporting conservation efforts, or advocating for sustainable policies. Let's work together to protect our home and preserve it for future generations."

Discovering the Importance of Saving and Preserving Our Environment"

Earth Collage: "Celebrate our Beautiful Planet"

Have students create a collage using recycled materials, depicting different aspects of the Earth, such as oceans, mountains, forests, and animals.

ᑭᑭᑭ

Recycled Art: "Reduce, Reuse, Recycle"

Have students use recycled materials to create a piece of art that represents the importance of reducing waste and taking care of our planet.

ᑭᑭᑭ

Plant a Garden: "Discover the Wonders of Nature"

Have students plant a garden and observe the growth of different plants, while learning about the importance of plants for our planet's health.

ᑭᑭᑭ

Earth Day Art: "Protect Our Planet"

Have students create a piece of art that celebrates Earth Day and promotes environmental awareness.

ᑭᑭᑭ

Nature Scavenger Hunt: "Explore the Wonders of Nature"

Take students on a nature scavenger hunt, looking for different plants, animals, and natural features, and have them create a drawing or painting of their favorite discovery.

ᑭᑭᑭ

Earth Quilt: "Piece Together Our Planet"

Have students create a quilt using different fabrics and colors that represent different parts of the Earth, such as continents, oceans, and natural features.

ᔕᔕᔕ

Weather Art: "Discover the Power of Nature"

Have students create a drawing or painting that depicts different types of weather, such as rain, snow, and thunderstorms, while learning about the science behind them.

ᔕᔕᔕ

Animal Habitat Art: "Protect Our Wildlife"

Have students create a piece of art that depicts the natural habitat of different animals, while learning about the importance of protecting wildlife and their habitats.

ᔕᔕᔕ

Water Conservation Art: "Save our Water, Save our Planet"

Have students create a piece of art that promotes water conservation and the importance of preserving our planet's water resources.

ᔕᔕᔕ

Solar System Art: "Our Home in the Universe"

Have students create a drawing or painting that shows the Earth as part of the solar system, while learning about the different planets and celestial bodies.

ᔕᔕᔕ

Remember to adapt the activities according to the age and interests of your students, and have fun exploring the wonders of our planet!

135

Dress to Impress, Every day

Style that suits you

The clothes we wear can say a lot about us, and they can also make us feel more confident and ready to take on the day. From casual jeans and t-shirts to elegant dresses and suits, there are many different types of clothes to choose from for any occasion. Whether you're dressing up for a special event or just want to feel your best at work or school, the right outfit can make all the difference.

Tie-Dye T-Shirts: "Get Groovy with Tie-Dye! Learn Colors, Patterns, and Creativity"

ᐅᐅᐅ

Sock Puppets: "Sock it to Me! Make your own Puppet Pal and Tell a Story"

ᚦᚦᚦ

Paper Bag Hats: "Hats off to Imagination! Make a Hat and Explore your Creativity"

ᚦᚦᚦ

Fabric Collage: "Piece Together your Imagination! Make a Collage with Different Fabrics"

ᚦᚦᚦ

T-Shirt Stamping: "Stamp your Style! Learn Printing and Design on T-Shirts"

ᚦᚦᚦ

Button Art: "Button Up Your Imagination! Make Art with Buttons and Learn about Colors and Shapes"

ᚦᚦᚦ

Fabric Painting: "Paint the Town with Color! Learn Painting Techniques on Fabric"

ᚦᚦᚦ

Recycled Clothes Crafts: "Reduce, Reuse, and Recreate! Make Art from Old Clothes and Learn about Sustainability"

ᚦᚦᚦ

Hat Decorating: "Top Off your Creativity! Decorate your Hat and Learn about Fashion and Design"

ᚦᚦᚦ

Bead Jewelry: "Beads of Fun! Make Jewelry and Learn about Patterns and Shapes"

ᚦᚦᚦ

Friendship Bracelets: "Wear your Heart on your Wrist! Make a Friendship Bracelet and Learn about Kindness"

ᚦᚦᚦ

Handprint Shirts: "Leave your Mark! Make a Handprint Shirt and Learn about Self-Expression"

❥❥❥

Felt Finger Puppets: "Felt like Making Puppets? Create a Cast of Characters and Learn about Storytelling"

❥❥❥

Denim Upcycling: "Jeans Genius! Transform Old Denim into Something New and Learn about Sustainability"

❥❥❥

Paper Plate Masks: "Masks on, Imagination Unleashed! Make a Mask and Explore your Creativity"

❥❥❥

Ribbon Wands: "Wave your Magic Wand! Make a Ribbon Wand and Learn about Movement and Dance"

❥❥❥

Applique Tote Bags: "Sew Much Fun! Create a Tote Bag and Learn about Sewing and Design"

❥❥❥

Sun Hats: "Sun's Out, Hats On! Make a Hat and Learn about Sun Safety and Fashion"

❥❥❥

Shoelace Weaving: "Tie it Up! Weave your Shoelaces and Learn about Patterns and Texture"

❥❥❥

Colorful Scarves: "Wrap Up your Creativity! Dye a Scarf and Learn about Color Mixing and Textile Design"

❥❥❥

136

Matter Matters - in all its States!

Changing states, changing worlds

The matter is all around us, and it can exist in three different states: solid, liquid, and gas. Each state has its own unique properties and characteristics, and understanding these states is crucial to understanding the world we live in. Solids have a definite shape and volume, while liquids take the shape of their container but have a definite volume, and gases have neither a definite shape nor volume. By studying the properties of matter in its various states, scientists can make new discoveries and improve our daily lives in countless ways.

Ice Cream in a Bag: "Scoops of Fun! Make Ice Cream and Learn about Freezing and Melting"

Oobleck Exploration: "Messy, but Fun! Experiment with Oobleck and Learn about Liquids and Solids"

Dancing Raisins: "Raisin the Roof! Make Raisins Dance and Learn about Gas and Buoyancy" (Details given separately)

Balloon Blow-Up: "Blow it Up! Inflate Balloons and Learn about Air and Pressure"

Cloud in a Jar: "Cloud Nine! Create a Cloud in a Jar and Learn about Condensation and Evaporation"

Marshmallow Molecules: "Sweet Science! Make Molecules with Marshmallows and Learn about the States of Matter"

Solid, Liquid, Gas Art: "Art Attack! Create Art with Different States of Matter and Learn about Properties"

DIY Lava Lamp: "Let it Flow! Make a Lava Lamp and Learn about Density and Viscosity"

Melting Crayons: "Melt Away Stress! Create Art with Melted Crayons and Learn about Melting Points"

Bubble Science: "Bubbling with Excitement! Experiment with Bubbles and Learn about Surface Tension and Gas"

Salt Crystal Snowflakes: "Frozen in Time! Make Salt Crystals and Learn about Crystallization and Solidification"

Water Cycle Collage: "Water, Water Everywhere! Create a Collage and Learn about the Water Cycle and States of Matter"

Jello Sensory Play: "Jiggly Science! Play with Jello and Learn about Gels and Liquids"

Vinegar and Baking Soda Volcanoes: "Erupting with Fun! Create a Volcano and Learn about Chemical Reactions and Gas"

DIY Slime: "Slime Time! Make Slime and Learn about Polymers and Viscosity"

Milk Art: "Colorful Chemistry! Experiment with Milk and Learn about Surface Tension and Chemical Reactions"

Magnetic Putty: "Putty Magic! Play with Magnetic Putty and Learn about Magnetism and Polymers"

Paper Snowflakes: "Cut it Out! Create Paper Snowflakes and Learn about Symmetry and Crystallization"

Frozen Paint Art: "Cool Art! Freeze Paint and Learn about Freezing and Melting Points"

137

Precision Counts, Measure Twice

Measure up to your potential

In many areas of life, precision is key. Whether you're building a house, baking a cake, or analyzing data, accurate measurements are essential to getting the results you want. From rulers and scales to more advanced tools like lasers and spectrometers, there are many different ways to measure the things that matter most. By taking the time to measure twice and ensure your measurements are accurate, you can avoid costly mistakes and achieve the precision you need to succeed.

Paper Airplane Distance Challenge: "Take Flight! Measure Distance with Paper Airplanes and Learn about Units of Measurement"

Water Bottle Rocket Launch: "3, 2, 1, Blastoff! Measure Distance with Water Bottle Rockets and Learn about Measuring Speed and Distance"

DIY Balance Scale: "Balancing Act! Make a Balance Scale and Learn about Weights and Measures"

Nature Walk Scavenger Hunt: "Explore and Measure! Take a Nature Walk and Learn about Measuring Length and Height

Build a Fort: "Fort Building Fun! Measure and Build a Fort and Learn about Measuring Angles and Shapes"

DIY Thermometer: "Temperature Check! Make a Thermometer and Learn about Measuring Temperature"

Lego Measurement Challenge: "Lego Mania! Measure and Build with Legos and Learn about Units of Measurement"

Measure Up: "Size Matters! Measure Everyday Objects and Learn about Measuring Length, Width and Height"

Liquid Measurement Relay: "Liquid Race! Measure and Pour Liquid in a Relay and Learn about Measuring Volume"

Scale Drawing Art: "Draw to Scale! Create Art with Scale Drawing and Learn about Ratios and Proportions"

Bean Bag Toss: "Aim and Measure! Measure Distance with Bean Bag Toss and Learn about Units of Measurement"

DIY Ruler: "Measure Twice, Cut Once! Make a Ruler and Learn about Measuring Length and Inches"

Cooking and Baking: "Kitchen Fun! Measure Ingredients and Learn about Units of Measurement"

Shape and Pattern Hunt: "Find the Shapes! Measure and Hunt for Shapes and Learn about Geometric Shapes"

Marble Run Challenge: "Rolling Fun! Measure Time with Marble Runs and Learn about Measuring Speed and Distance"

Geocaching: "Find the Treasure! Measure Distance and Hunt for Geocaches and Learn about GPS and Coordinates"

Puzzle Building Challenge: "Puzzle Time! Measure and Build Puzzles and Learn about Measuring Angles and Shapes"

Garden Measuring: "Green Thumb! Measure and Plant a Garden and Learn about Measuring Length, Width and Height"

DIY Clock: "Time Keeper! Make a Clock and Learn about Measuring Time"

Shape Collage Art: "Shape Up! Create Art with Shapes and Learn about Measuring Area and Perimeter"

138
Home is where the Heart is, No Matter the Type

Building dreams, one home at a time

Homes come in all shapes and sizes, from tiny apartments to sprawling mansions, and each type has its own unique charm and appeal. Whether you live in a cozy cottage, a modern condo, or a rustic farmhouse, the place you call home is where you can relax, unwind, and be yourself. With so many different types of homes to choose from, there's something out there for everyone.

Build a Dream House: "House of Your Dreams! Design and Build Your Dream House and Learn about Architectural Styles"

Fairy House Building: "Magical Houses! Build Fairy Houses and Learn about Different Types of Dwellings"

Lego House Challenge: "Lego Mania! Build Houses with Legos and Learn about Building Materials and Designs"

Recycled Material House: "Green Building! Build Houses with Recycled Materials and Learn about Sustainability and Eco-friendly Houses"

Paper House Art: "Paper Power! Create Art with Paper Houses and Learn about Different Types of Homes"

Gingerbread House Decorating: "Sweet Houses! Decorate Gingerbread Houses and Learn about Building Materials and Designs"

Puppet House Play: "Puppet House Fun! Build and Play with Puppet Houses and Learn about Different Types of Dwellings"

Shape House Collage: "Shape Up! Create Art with Shapes and Learn about Different Types of Houses and Building Designs"

Minecraft House Design: "Game On! Design and Build Houses in Minecraft and Learn about Architectural Styles and Materials"

Shoebox Diorama Houses: "3D Houses! Create Shoebox Diorama Houses and Learn about Different Types of Homes and Building Materials"

Shadow Puppet House Theater: "Shadow Houses! Create a Puppet House Theater and Learn about Different Types of Dwellings and Light and Shadow"

Play-Doh House Sculpture: "Sculpting Fun! Create Play-Doh House Sculptures and Learn about Building Materials and Designs"

Monopoly House Building: "Build Your Property! Design and Build Houses in Monopoly and Learn about Architectural Styles and Building Materials"

Dollhouse Decorating: "Tiny Houses! Decorate Dollhouses and Learn about Different Types of Homes and Building Styles"

Clay House Building: "Pottery Power! Build Houses with Clay and Learn about Building Materials and Designs"

House Drawing Challenge: "Drawing Houses! Sketch Different Types of Houses and Learn about Architectural Styles and Building Materials"

Virtual House Tours: "House Tours! Take Virtual Tours of Different Types of Homes and Learn about Building Styles and Materials"

Storybook House Illustration: "Illustrate a Storybook House! Create Art with Storybook Houses and Learn about Building Materials and Designs"

Pop-up House Card Making: "Pop-up Fun! Create House Pop-up Cards and Learn about Different Types of Homes and Building Designs"

Building Block House Challenge: "Block by Block! Build Houses with Building Blocks and Learn about Building Materials and Designs"

139

Illuminate your World, Amplify your Voice

See the Light, Hear the Sound

Light and sound are powerful tools that can be used to illuminate and amplify the world around us. Whether you're using light to brighten a room, create a work of art, or explore the depths of the universe, or using sound to share your message, entertain an audience, or connect with others, the possibilities are endless. By understanding the physics of light and sound and mastering their use, you can illuminate your world and amplify your voice like never before.

Shadow Play Theater: "Shadow Fun! Create a Shadow Play Theater and Learn about Light and Shadow"

Musical Instrument Making: "Make Some Noise! Build Musical Instruments and Learn about Sound Waves"

Kaleidoscope Making: "Kaleidoscope Fun! Create Your Own Kaleidoscopes and Learn about Reflection and Light"

Sound Wave Art: "Art of Sound! Create Art with Sound Waves and Learn about Frequency and Pitch"

Prism Experiment: "Rainbow Magic! Conduct Prism Experiments and Learn about Refraction and Light"

DIY Speaker Building: "Amplify Your Sound! Build DIY Speakers and Learn about Sound Waves and Vibration"

Flashlight Shadow Drawing: "Shadow Play! Draw with Flashlights and Learn about Light and Shadow"

Sound Map Creation: "Mapping Sounds! Create a Sound Map and Learn about Sound Waves and Frequency"

Light Painting Art: "Painting with Light! Create Art with Light and Learn about Light and Colors"

Laser Maze Game: "Laser Fun! Play Laser Maze Game and Learn about Light Reflection and Refraction"

Sound Scavenger Hunt: "Hunting for Sound! Go on a Sound Scavenger Hunt and Learn about Sound Waves and Frequency"

Light Refraction Experiment: "Bending Light! Conduct Light Refraction Experiment and Learn about Reflection and Refraction"

Musical Painting: "Musical Art! Create Art with Music and Learn about Sound Waves and Frequency"

Laser Light Show: "Laser Spectacular! Create a Laser Light Show and Learn about Light and Colors"

DIY Microphone Building: "Sound Engineering! Build DIY Microphones and Learn about Sound Waves and Vibration"

Rainbow Spin Art: "Rainbow Spin! Create Art with Rainbow Spin Art and Learn about Colors and Light"

Sound Matching Game: "Matching Sounds! Play Sound Matching Game and Learn about Sound Waves and Frequency"

Light Box Art: "Light Box Fun! Create Art with Light Boxes and Learn about Light and Shadow"

Musical Water Glasses: "Music in a Glass! Play Musical Water Glasses and Learn about Sound Waves and Vibration"

UV Light Experiment: "Invisible Light! Conduct UV Light Experiment and Learn about Ultraviolet Light and Light Spectrum"

140

Birds of a feather, with beaks that flock together

Feathered friends with Unique Beaks

Birds come in all shapes and sizes, with beaks that are as diverse as their plumage. Whether it's the sharp, hooked beak of a raptor or the long, slender beak of a shorebird, each bird's beak is perfectly adapted to its unique needs and habitat. Birds also have other distinctive features, such as feathers that keep them warm and help them fly, and specialized feet that enable them to perch, grasp, or wade in water. By observing and learning about the fascinating adaptations of birds, we can gain a greater appreciation for the complexity and beauty of the natural world.

Birdhouse Building: "Build a Birdhouse! Create Birdhouses and Learn about Different Types of Birds and Their Habitats"

Feather Art: "Feather Fun! Create Art with Feathers and Learn about Different Types of Birds and Their Features"

Beak Adaptations Experiment: "Beak Adaptations! Conduct Experiments on Bird Beaks and Learn about Different Types of Birds and Their Adaptations"

Bird Watching Field Trip: "Bird Watching Adventure! Go on a Bird Watching Field Trip and Learn about Different Types of Birds and Their Habitats"

Wing Design Challenge: "Wing It! Design and Build Wings and Learn about Different Types of Birds and Their Flight"

Bird Song Identification: "Listen and Learn! Identify Bird Songs and Learn about Different Types of Birds and Their Sounds"

Feather Sorting Activity: "Sorting Feathers! Sort Feathers and Learn about Different Types of Birds and Their Features"

Bird Beak Scavenger Hunt: "Beak Hunt! Go on a Scavenger Hunt for Different Types of Bird Beaks and Learn about Their Adaptations"

Bird Drawing Challenge: "Draw a Bird! Sketch Different Types of Birds and Learn about Their Features and Characteristics"

Bird Origami: "Origami Birds! Create Origami Birds and Learn about Different Types of Birds and Their Features and Behaviours"

Bird Nest Building: "Build a Nest! Create Bird Nests and Learn about Different Types of Birds and Their Nesting Habits"

Bird Migration Maps: "Follow the Flock! Create Bird Migration Maps and Learn about Different Types of Birds and Their Migratory Patterns"

Bird Photography Contest: "Snap a Bird! Take Photos of Different Types of Birds and Learn about Their Features and Behaviors"

Bird Wing Anatomy: "Wing Anatomy! Dissect **fallen** Bird Wings and Learn about Their Structure and Function" **Don't harm animals/birds/**

anyone.

Bird Beak Measurement: "Beak Measurement! Measure Different Types of Bird Beaks and Learn about Their Adaptations"

Bird Feather Collage: "Feather Collage! Create Collages with Different Types of Bird Feathers and Learn about Their Features and Colors"

Bird Habitat Diorama: "Habitat Diorama! Create Dioramas of Different Types of Bird Habitats and Learn about Their Ecosystems"

Bird Drawing Tutorial: "Draw Like a Pro! Follow Bird Drawing Tutorials and Learn about Different Types of Birds and Their Features"

Bird Watching Bingo: "Bird Bingo! Play Bingo while Bird Watching and Learn about Different Types of Birds and Their Behaviors"

Bird Watching Journal: "Bird Journal! Create Journals while Bird Watching and Learn about Different Types of Birds and Their Characteristics"

141

Seasons Change, but the Weather Remains

Weather the storm, embrace the seasons

The changing of the seasons is one of the most awe-inspiring phenomena in the natural world, and it's all driven by the changing weather patterns that accompany each season. From the bright colours of autumn leaves to the lush greenery of springtime blooms, each season brings its own unique beauty and wonder. By paying attention to the weather and the changing of the seasons, we can learn to appreciate the cyclical nature of life and find joy in the ebb and flow of the natural world.

Weather Art: "Weather Wonders! Create Art Inspired by Different Types of Weather and Learn about the Seasons"

Weather Journaling: "Weather Reporter! Keep a Weather Journal and Learn about the Different Seasons"

Seasonal Tree Art: "Tree Seasons! Create Art of Trees in Different Seasons and Learn about the Changes in Weather"

Weather Dramatization: "Weather Plays! Act Out Different Weather Scenarios and Learn about Weather Patterns"

Weather Songs: "Sing a Song! Create Weather Songs and Learn about the Different Seasons"

Seasonal Clothing Design: "Fashion Forecast! Design Clothes for Different Seasons and Learn about Weather Changes"

Weather Instruments Experiment: "Weather Instruments! Conduct Experiments with Weather Instruments and Learn about Weather Measurements"

Seasonal Collages: "Collage Seasons! Create Collages of Different Seasons and Learn about Weather Changes"

Seasonal Bookmarks: "Bookmarks for Seasons! Create Bookmarks for Different Seasons and Learn about Weather Changes"

Seasonal Poetry: "Poetic Seasons! Write Poems about Different Seasons and Learn about Weather Changes"

Weather Diorama: "Weather World! Create Dioramas of Different Weather Conditions and Learn about the Seasons"

Seasonal Mobiles: "Mobile Seasons! Create Mobiles of Different Seasons and Learn about Weather Patterns"

Weather Sketching: "Sketching Weather! Sketch Different Weather Conditions and Learn about the Seasons"

Weather Puzzles: "Puzzle Weather! Solve Puzzles about Different Weather Conditions and Learn about the Seasons"

Seasonal Storytelling: "Storytelling Seasons! Tell Stories about Different Seasons and Learn about the Weather Patterns"

Weather Photography: "Weather Photography! Take Photos of Different Weather Conditions and Learn about the Seasons"

Weather Charades: "Charades Weather! Play Charades about Different Weather Conditions and Learn about the Seasons"

Seasonal Posters: "Posters for Seasons! Create Posters about Different Seasons and Learn about the Weather Patterns"

Weather Bingo: "Weather Bingo! Play Bingo with Different Weather Conditions and Learn about the Seasons"

Seasonal Paintings: "Painting Seasons! Paint Different Seasons and Learn about the Changes in Weather"

142
Safety First, Care Always

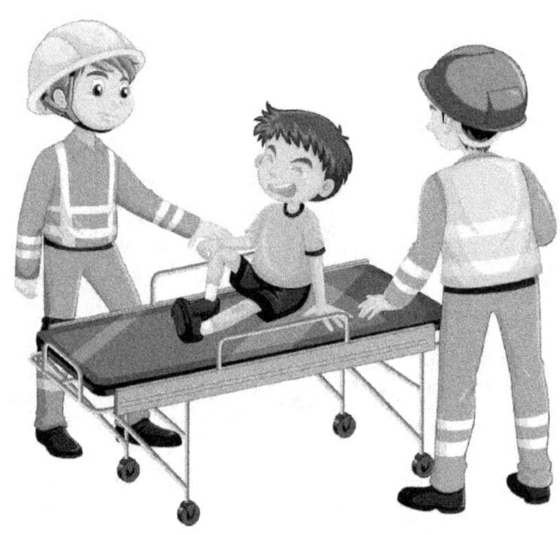

Be prepared, save a life

Safety is a critical component of living a healthy and fulfilling life, and it's something that we should all take seriously. From wearing a seatbelt in the car to using protective gear while playing sports, there are many ways to reduce our risk of injury and stay safe. However, accidents and injuries can still happen, and that's where first aid comes in. By learning basic first aid skills and knowing how to respond in an emergency, we can help ourselves and others when accidents do occur.

Safety Posters: "Safety First! Create Posters on Safety and Learn about First Aid"

First Aid Dramatization: "First Aid Act! Dramatize First Aid Scenarios and Learn about Safety"

Safety Songs: "Sing Safety! Create Safety Songs and Learn about First Aid"

Safety Bookmarks: "Bookmark Safety! Create Bookmarks on Safety and Learn about First Aid"

Safety Charades: "Charades Safety! Play Charades on Safety and Learn about First Aid"

Safety Poetry: "Poetic Safety! Write Poems on Safety and Learn about First Aid"

Safety Collages: "Collage Safety! Create Collages on Safety and Learn about First Aid"

Safety Bracelets: "Safety Bracelets! Make Bracelets on Safety and Learn about First Aid"

Safety Puppet Show: "Puppet Safety! Put on a Puppet Show on Safety and Learn about First Aid"

Safety Diorama: "Safety World! Create Dioramas on Safety and Learn about First Aid"

Safety Comics: "Comic Safety! Create Comics on Safety and Learn about First Aid"

First Aid Collages: "Collage First Aid! Create Collages on First Aid Techniques and Learn about Safety"

Safety Games: "Game Safety! Create Games on Safety and Learn about First Aid"

First Aid Posters: "First Aid Alert! Create Posters on First Aid Techniques and Learn about Safety"

Safety Dance: "Safety Boogie! Choreograph a Dance Routine on Safety and Learn about First Aid"

First Aid Treasure Hunt: "Treasure First Aid! Go on a Treasure Hunt for First Aid Supplies and Learn about Safety"

Safety Quilts: "Quilt Safety! Create Quilts on Safety and Learn about First Aid"

First Aid Bracelets: "First Aid Bracelets! Make Bracelets on First Aid Techniques and Learn about Safety"

Safety Theater: "Theater Safety! Perform a Play on Safety and Learn about First Aid"

First Aid Mural: "Mural First Aid! Create a Mural on First Aid Techniques and Learn about Safety"

143

Details on Some Activities/Experiments

Refer to the next few pages for details on some uncommon activities/experiments.

Dancing Raisins

"Dancing Raisins" is a fun and simple science experiment that teaches about gas and buoyancy. Here are the details on how to conduct this experiment:

Materials needed:

- Clear glass or plastic container (e.g., a tall drinking glass)
- Raisins (3-4)
- Baking soda
- Vinegar
- Water

Instructions:

- Fill the glass about 2/3 full with water.
- Add 1-2 tablespoons of baking soda to the water and stir until dissolved.
- Drop in 3-4 raisins.
- Pour in enough vinegar to cover the raisins.
- Observe the raisins as they begin to "dance" and float up to the surface, then sink back down to the bottom.

Explanation:

When the vinegar and baking soda mix together, they undergo a chemical reaction that produces carbon dioxide gas. The gas bubbles attach to the surface of the raisins, causing them to become buoyant and float to the surface of the liquid. When the raisins reach the surface, the gas bubbles pop and the raisins lose their buoyancy, causing them to sink back down to the bottom. The process repeats as more carbon dioxide gas is produced, creating the appearance of the raisins "dancing".

This experiment is a great way to teach children about the concepts of gas, buoyancy, and chemical reactions in a fun and interactive way.

৩৩৩

Oobleck Experiment

Oobleck is a non-Newtonian fluid made from a mixture of cornstarch and water. It is a fun and messy material that can be used to teach children about the properties of liquids and solids. Here are the details on how to conduct an Oobleck exploration experiment:

Materials needed:

- Cornstarch
- Water
- Large mixing bowl
- Spoon
- Food coloring (optional)
- Tray or container to contain the Oobleck

Instructions:

- In a large mixing bowl, combine 1 part water with 1.5-2 parts cornstarch. For example, use 1 cup of water with 1.5-2 cups of cornstarch.
- Mix the water and cornstarch together with a spoon until the mixture is smooth and has a thick, gooey consistency.
- Optional: add food coloring to the mixture to create different colors.
- Once the Oobleck is mixed, let children explore its properties. Encourage them to touch and play with it, noticing how it behaves differently than regular liquids or solids. Some suggestions for exploration include:
- Squeeze it in your hand and notice how it feels solid, but then flows out of your hand like a liquid when you release it.
- Try to roll it into a ball, but notice how it falls apart and becomes a liquid when you stop applying pressure.
- Place it on a tray or container and try to make designs or shapes by pressing it with your fingers or tools.
- Add more water or cornstarch to the mixture and notice how it affects the texture and behavior of the Oobleck.

Explanation:

Oobleck is a non-Newtonian fluid, which means it has properties of both liquids and solids. When pressure is applied to the Oobleck, it behaves like a solid and resists the force. But when the pressure is released, it flows like a liquid. This behavior is due to the interaction between the cornstarch particles and water molecules, which create a suspension that can change its viscosity based on the amount of pressure applied.

This experiment is a great way to teach children about the properties of non-Newtonian fluids and how they behave differently from regular liquids and solids. It also allows for hands-on exploration and creativity, making it a fun and engaging activity for children of all ages.

ppp

Jello Sensory Play

Jello sensory play is a fun and engaging activity that teaches children about the properties of gels and liquids. Here are the details on how to conduct a Jello sensory play experiment:

Materials needed:

- Jello mix (any flavor)
- Water
- Large mixing bowl
- Spoon
- Tray or container for the Jello
- Optional: toys or objects to hide in the Jello for a treasure hunt

Instructions:

- Prepare the Jello according to the package instructions, using hot water to dissolve the mix and cold water to set it.
- Pour the Jello mixture into a large mixing bowl.
- Let the Jello cool down to room temperature, stirring occasionally to prevent it from setting too quickly.
- Once the Jello has cooled down, transfer it to a tray or container for sensory play.
- Let children explore the Jello with their hands, noticing how it feels different from regular liquids or solids. Some suggestions for exploration include:
- Squeeze the Jello and notice how it jiggles and wobbles like a gel.
- Try to pick up pieces of the Jello and notice how they are soft and pliable.
- Hide small toys or objects in the Jello for a treasure hunt, encouraging children to use their sense of touch to find them.

Explanation:

Jello is a type of gel, which is a material that behaves like a solid and a liquid at the same time. Gels are made up of a network of interconnected molecules that give them their unique properties. In the case of Jello, the network is formed by gelatin molecules, which create a flexible and wobbly structure that is both solid and liquid at the same time.

This experiment is a great way to teach children about the properties of gels and how they differ from regular liquids or solids. It also allows for hands-on exploration and creativity, making it a fun and engaging activity for children of all ages.

ᗡᗡᗡ

Marshmallow Molecules

Marshmallow molecules is a fun and educational activity that teaches children about the states of matter and how they interact to form molecules. Here are the details on how to conduct a marshmallow molecules experiment:

Materials needed:

- Mini marshmallows
- Toothpicks
- Large tray or surface for building molecules
- Optional: diagrams or pictures of molecules for reference

Instructions:

- Start by showing children diagrams or pictures of simple molecules, such as water (H_2O) or carbon dioxide (CO_2), for reference.
- Distribute mini marshmallows and toothpicks to each child or group.
- Encourage children to use the marshmallows and toothpicks to build molecules on a large tray or surface. Some suggestions for building molecules include:
- Water (H_2O): use two marshmallows to represent the hydrogen atoms and one marshmallow to represent the oxygen atom, connecting them with toothpicks to form a triangle shape.
- Carbon dioxide (CO_2): use two marshmallows to represent the oxygen atoms and one toothpick to represent the carbon atom, connecting them in a straight line.
- Methane (CH_4): use four marshmallows to represent the hydrogen atoms and one marshmallow to represent the carbon atom, connecting them in a tetrahedral shape.
- Discuss with children the properties of the different states of matter and how they interact to form molecules. For example, oxygen and hydrogen are gases, while carbon is a solid, but they can combine to form water, which is a liquid.

Explanation:

Molecules are made up of atoms, which can be represented by the marshmallows in this experiment. The toothpicks represent the bonds between the atoms, which hold them together to form molecules. By building different molecules with marshmallows and toothpicks, children can see how the different states of matter (solid, liquid, and gas) interact to form different compounds and molecules.

This experiment is a great way to teach children about the properties of matter and how they interact to form different substances. It also allows for hands-on exploration and creativity, making it a fun and engaging activity for children of all ages.

Magnetic Putty

Magnetic putty is a fun and engaging activity that teaches children about the properties of polymers and magnetism. Here are the details on how to conduct a magnetic putty experiment:

Materials needed:

- Magnetic putty
- Strong magnets
- Optional: plastic or paper cups, plastic utensils for mixing, small objects to hide in the putty for a treasure hunt

Instructions:

- Start by showing children the properties of magnetic putty, which is a type of polymer that contains iron oxide particles that respond to magnets.
- Distribute magnetic putty to each child or group.
- Encourage children to experiment with the putty, noticing how it stretches, bounces, and reacts to magnets. Some suggestions for exploring magnetic putty include:
- Use the magnets to pick up the putty and move it around.
- Stretch and twist the putty, noticing how it changes shape and texture.
- Hide small objects in the putty for a treasure hunt, encouraging children to use the magnets to find them.
- Discuss with children the properties of polymers and how they differ from other types of materials. For example, polymers are made up of long chains of molecules that give them their unique properties, such as elasticity and flexibility.
- Discuss with children the properties of magnets and how they attract or repel certain materials, such as iron or nickel.

Explanation:

Magnetic putty is made up of a type of polymer that contains iron oxide particles. When exposed to a strong magnet, these particles align with the magnetic field, creating a temporary magnetic charge in the putty. This allows the putty to respond to the magnet, allowing children to experiment with the properties of magnetism in a fun and interactive way.

This experiment is a great way to teach children about the properties of polymers and how they interact with other materials, as well as the properties of magnetism and how it can be used to manipulate certain materials. It also allows for hands-on exploration and creativity, making it a fun and engaging activity for children of all ages.

▷▷▷

Frozen Paint Art

Frozen paint art is a fun and creative activity that teaches children about the properties of freezing and melting points. Here are the details on how to conduct a frozen paint art experiment:

Materials needed:

- Tempera paint or food coloring
- Water
- Ice cube trays or small cups
- Popsicle sticks or plastic spoons
- Paper or cardboard for painting on

Instructions:

- Start by mixing tempera paint or food coloring with water in a small cup or ice cube tray. You can use as many colors as you like.
- Place the cups or ice cube tray in the freezer and freeze until solid.
- Once the paint is frozen, remove it from the cups or ice cube tray and let it thaw for a few minutes.
- Use the popsicle sticks or plastic spoons to mix and spread the thawed paint onto paper or cardboard, creating a unique frozen paint art piece.
- Observe and discuss with children the changes in the paint as it freezes and thaws, and how this relates to the properties of freezing and melting points.

Explanation:

Freezing and melting points are the temperatures at which a substance transitions from a liquid to a solid or from a solid to a liquid, respectively. By freezing the paint, children can observe how the water molecules in the paint solidify and how they return to a liquid state when the paint thaws. This experiment also allows children to explore the properties of color mixing, as they can mix different colors together in the ice cube tray to create new hues in their frozen paint art.

This experiment is a great way to teach children about the properties of freezing and melting points and how they relate to the states of matter (solid, liquid, and gas). It also encourages creativity and artistic expression, making it a fun and engaging activity for children of all ages.

ᗑᗑᗑ

Bean Bag Toss

Bean bag toss is a fun game that can be used to teach children about units of measurement and distance. Here are the details on how to conduct a bean bag toss experiment:

Materials needed:

- Bean bags
- Measuring tape or ruler
- Marker or chalk for marking distances
- Optional: targets or hoops for aiming at

Instructions:

- Set up the targets or hoops at different distances from the starting line. Use a measuring tape or ruler to measure the distance from the starting line to each target, and mark the distance with a marker or chalk.
- Give each child or group a set of bean bags.
- Explain to children that they will be measuring the distance they are able to throw the bean bag, and that they will be using units of measurement such as feet or meters.
- Encourage children to take turns throwing the bean bag towards the targets, measuring the distance it travels each time. Have them record their distances on a chart or graph.
- Discuss with children the different units of measurement they used and how they relate to each other. For example, one foot is equivalent to 12 inches or 0.3 meters.
- Encourage children to practice their aim and to see if they can improve their distances over time.

Explanation:

Measuring distance is an important skill that children will use throughout their lives. By using a fun and engaging activity like bean bag toss, children can practice measuring distance while also having fun and improving their aim. This experiment also teaches children about units of measurement and how they relate to each other, helping them to develop a basic understanding of measurement and the importance of accuracy in measuring.

This experiment is a great way to teach children about units of measurement and distance, as well as improving their hand-eye coordination and aim. It also encourages friendly competition and teamwork, making it a fun and engaging activity for children of all ages.

ᗡᗡᗡ

Monopoly house building

Monopoly house building is a fun and educational activity that allows children to learn about architectural styles and building materials while also practicing their creativity and problem-solving skills. Here are the details on how to conduct a Monopoly house building experiment:

Materials needed:

- Monopoly game board
- Monopoly houses and hotels
- Drawing materials (paper, pencils, markers, etc.)
- Optional: reference books or online resources on architectural styles and building materials

Instructions:

- Start by playing a game of Monopoly with the children, or use a pre-set game board.
- After each player has acquired some properties, explain that they can now start building houses on their properties.
- Encourage the children to research different architectural styles and building materials, using reference books or online resources if available.
- Have the children draw and design their own houses, incorporating different architectural styles and building materials into their designs. They can use Monopoly houses and hotels as a starting point for their designs or create their own designs from scratch.
- Encourage the children to use their creativity and problem-solving skills to overcome any design challenges that arise, such as limited space or a specific architectural style requirement.
- After the children have designed their houses, have them present their designs to the group and explain their architectural style and building materials choices.

Explanation:

This activity allows children to learn about different architectural styles and building materials, as well as the design process and problem-solving skills. It also encourages creativity and allows children to express themselves through their designs. By incorporating Monopoly houses and hotels into the activity, children can also practice their counting and math skills as they determine how many houses they can afford to build on each property.

Overall, Monopoly house building is a fun and educational activity that can be enjoyed by children of all ages. It provides an opportunity for children to learn about architecture and design while also having fun and practicing their creativity and problem-solving skills.

ᐅᐅᐅ

Musical Painting

Musical painting is a fun and interactive activity that allows children to explore the relationship between music and art while learning about sound waves and frequency. Here are the details on how to conduct a musical painting experiment:

Materials needed:

- Paint
- Paint brushes
- Paper or canvas
- Speakers or music player
- Optional: music with different frequencies, such as classical or electronic music

Instructions:

- Set up the painting area with paper or canvas, paint, and paint brushes.
- Turn on the music player or speakers and play music with different frequencies, such as classical or electronic music. Explain to the children that different sounds have different frequencies, which can affect how we perceive the sound.
- Encourage the children to paint along with the music, using the brush strokes and colors to reflect the rhythm and mood of the music.
- Ask the children to experiment with different types of music and observe how it affects their painting style and mood.
- Discuss with the children the relationship between sound waves and frequency, and how it can affect our perception of music and art.

Explanation:

Musical painting allows children to explore the relationship between music and art while also learning about sound waves and frequency. By painting along with music, children can learn to express themselves through art and music, while also developing an understanding of how sound waves and frequency affect our perception of music and art.

This activity can also help children develop their listening skills and improve their coordination between sound and movement. By experimenting with different types of music, children can also learn to appreciate different styles of music and how they can affect our emotions and moods.

Overall, musical painting is a fun and educational activity that can be enjoyed by children of all ages. It provides an opportunity for children to learn about sound waves and frequency while also expressing themselves through art and music.

♭♭♭

Musical Water Glasses

Musical water glasses is a fun and educational activity that teaches children about sound waves and vibration while also allowing them to create their own music. Here are the details on how to conduct a musical water glasses experiment:

Materials needed:

- Water glasses
- Water
- Food coloring (optional)
- Spoon or mallet

Instructions:

- Fill the water glasses with different amounts of water, leaving some glasses empty and some glasses full.
- Optional: add food coloring to each glass to make them more visually appealing.
- Use a spoon or mallet to gently tap each glass and observe the different sounds it makes.
- Encourage the children to experiment with tapping the glasses in different ways, such as using the back of the spoon or tapping the side of the glass.
- Have the children try to play a simple tune by tapping the glasses in a specific order.
- Discuss with the children the relationship between sound waves and vibration, and how it affects the sound produced by the glasses.

Explanation:

Musical water glasses is a fun and educational activity that teaches children about sound waves and vibration. By tapping the glasses, children can observe how different amounts of water produce different sounds and pitches. They can also experiment with different tapping techniques to create their own music.

This activity can help children develop their listening skills and improve their coordination between sound and movement. By learning about the relationship between sound waves and vibration, children can also gain an understanding of how sound is produced and how it travels through the air.

Overall, musical water glasses is a fun and educational activity that can be enjoyed by children of all ages. It provides an opportunity for children to learn about sound waves and vibration while also creating their own music.

ᗊᗊᗊ

Bird Watching Bingo

Bird Watching Bingo is a fun and educational activity that combines the excitement of bingo with the outdoor adventure of bird watching. Here are the details on how to conduct a Bird Watching Bingo game:

Materials needed:

- Bingo cards with pictures of different types of birds
- Binoculars
- Field guide to identify different types of birds (optional)

Instructions:

- Distribute bingo cards with pictures of different types of birds to each player.
- Choose a location for bird watching, such as a local park or nature reserve.
- Use binoculars to spot different types of birds and mark them off on the bingo card.
- Discuss with the children the behaviors and characteristics of each bird as they are spotted.
- The first player to get bingo by spotting all the birds on their card wins the game.
- Optional: use a field guide to identify the different types of birds and learn more about their behaviors and habitats.

Explanation:

Bird Watching Bingo is a fun and educational activity that allows children to learn about different types of birds and their behaviors while playing a game of bingo. By using binoculars to spot birds and identify them on the bingo card, children can develop their observation skills and learn about different species of birds and their habitats.

This activity can also help children develop an appreciation for nature and the environment. By discussing the behaviors and characteristics of each bird as they are spotted, children can learn about the importance of preserving natural habitats and protecting wildlife.

Overall, Bird Watching Bingo is a fun and educational activity that can be enjoyed by children of all ages. It provides an opportunity for children to learn about different types of birds and their behaviors while also enjoying the outdoors and playing a fun game of bingo.

ᐁᐁᐁ

Weather Bingo

Weather Bingo is a fun and educational activity that teaches children about different weather conditions and the changing of seasons. Here are the details on how to conduct a Weather Bingo game:

Materials needed:

- Bingo cards with pictures of different weather conditions (such as rain, snow, thunderstorms, etc.)
  - Bingo chips or markers

Instructions:

- Distribute bingo cards with pictures of different weather conditions to each player.
  - Assign a caller to draw and call out the different weather conditions.
  - Players mark off the corresponding weather condition on their bingo card.
  - The first player to get bingo by marking off five in a row (horizontal, vertical, or diagonal) wins the game.
  - Discuss with the children the different weather conditions and how they relate to the changing of seasons.

Explanation:

Weather Bingo is a fun and educational activity that teaches children about different weather conditions and the changing of seasons. By playing the game, children can develop their observation skills and learn to recognize and identify different types of weather. They can also learn about the relationship between weather conditions and the changing of seasons.

This activity can also help children develop an appreciation for the environment and the importance of weather patterns in our daily lives. By discussing the different weather conditions and how they affect our daily activities, children can learn to plan and prepare for different weather events.

Overall, Weather Bingo is a fun and educational activity that can be enjoyed by children of all ages. It provides an opportunity for children to learn about different weather conditions and the changing of seasons while also playing a fun game of bingo.

ᗒᗒᗒ

Safety Diorama

Safety Diorama is an interactive and educational activity that allows children to create dioramas on safety and learn about first aid. Here are the details on how to conduct a Safety Diorama activity:

Materials needed:

Art supplies (such as cardboard, paper, scissors, glue, markers, etc.)

Toy figures and props (such as cars, houses, trees, etc.)

First aid kit (optional)

Instructions:

- Discuss with the children the importance of safety and first aid in our daily lives.
- Assign each child to create a diorama on safety using the art supplies and toy figures and props provided.
- Encourage the children to include different safety scenarios in their diorama, such as a car accident, a kitchen fire, or a fall.
- Once the dioramas are complete, discuss with the children the different safety scenarios depicted and the importance of first aid in each situation.
- Optional: use the first aid kit to demonstrate how to apply basic first aid techniques, such as bandaging a wound or treating a burn.

Explanation:

Safety Diorama is an interactive and educational activity that teaches children about safety and first aid. By creating dioramas on different safety scenarios, children can develop their creativity and problem-solving skills while also learning about the importance of safety and first aid in our daily lives.

This activity can also help children learn about the different types of injuries and how to prevent them. By discussing the different safety scenarios depicted in the dioramas, children can learn about the common causes of accidents and how to avoid them. They can also learn about basic first aid techniques and how to respond in case of an emergency.

Overall, Safety Diorama is a fun and educational activity that can be enjoyed by children of all ages. It provides an opportunity for children to learn about safety and first aid while also expressing their creativity and imagination.

ᗞᗞᗞ

144

Project 1: Plant a Garden for a Sustainable Future

Title: "Green Thumbs for a Greener Future": Planting the Seeds of Sustainability in Our Community

Grade level: Primary School (Grade 1-5)

Project Duration: 2-3 Weeks

SDG Goal: SDG 2 - Zero Hunger and SDG 15 - Life on Land

Project Overview:

- In this project, students will learn about the importance of plants, their role in our lives, and their impact on the environment.
- They will also explore various types of plants, their growth cycle, and their uses.
- The project will be integrated with different subjects like Math, English, Hindi, Social Studies, Value Education, Sports, and Information Technology.
- Students will also participate in a gardening activity, where they will plant their own garden and learn about sustainable agriculture practices.

Learning Outcomes:
Math:

- Students will be able to estimate and measure the area of their garden
- Students will be able to calculate the amount of soil and water required for their plants

English:

- Students will be able to write descriptive paragraphs about different plants
- Students will be able to create posters or flyers to promote their garden
- Students will be able to write journal entries about their gardening experiences

Hindi:

- Students will be able to learn and identify the names of different plants and their uses in Hindi
- Students will be able to write Hindi poems or songs about plants

Social Studies:

- Students will be able to understand the history of agriculture and its impact on society
- Students will be able to understand the impact of modern farming practices on the environment
- Students will be able to understand the role of farmers in our society

Value Education:

- Students will be able to understand the importance of sustainability and responsible consumption
- Students will be able to understand the importance of protecting the environment and preserving biodiversity

Sports:

- Students will be able to participate in physical activities related to gardening such as digging, planting, and watering
- Students will be able to understand the health benefits of eating fresh fruits and vegetables

Information Technology:

- Students will be able to create digital presentations about their garden and share them with their classmates
- Students will be able to use technology to research different plants and sustainable agriculture practices

Subjects Integration:

- Math - Students can learn about measuring and estimating the area of their garden. They can also calculate the amount of soil and water required for their plants.
- English - Students can write descriptive paragraphs about different plants, create posters or flyers to promote their garden, and write journal entries about their gardening experiences.
- Hindi - Students can learn the names of different plants and their uses in Hindi. They can also write Hindi poems or songs about plants.
- Social Studies - Students can learn about the history of agriculture, the role of farmers in our society, and the impact of modern farming practices on the environment.
- Value Education - Students can learn about the value of sustainability and responsible consumption. They can also learn about the importance of protecting the environment and preserving biodiversity.
- Sports - Students can participate in physical activities related to gardening, like digging, planting, and watering. They can also learn about the health benefits of eating fresh fruits and vegetables.
- Information Technology - Students can create digital presentations about their garden and share them with their classmates. They can also use technology to research different plants and sustainable agriculture practices.

Final Outcome:

The final integrated outcome of the "Green Thumbs for a Greener Future" project is a comprehensive understanding of the importance of plants, their impact on the environment, and the role of sustainable agriculture practices in building a better future for our community.

Through this project, students will have the opportunity to integrate different subjects like Math, English, Hindi, Social Studies, Value Education, Sports, and Information Technology to create a meaningful and engaging learning experience.

They will learn about measuring and estimating the area of their garden, calculating the amount of soil and water required for their plants, writing descriptive paragraphs and creating posters or flyers to promote their garden, learning the names and uses of different plants in Hindi, understanding the history of agriculture, the role of farmers in our society, the impact of modern farming practices on the environment, the importance of sustainability and responsible consumption, and the health benefits of eating fresh fruits and vegetables.

The final integrated outcome of the project will be a complete and well-designed garden, showcasing the students' creativity and innovation, understanding of different plants and their uses, and knowledge of sustainable agriculture practices. In addition, students will have developed a deeper appreciation for nature and a sense of responsibility towards the environment and learn how different subjects can be integrated to create a comprehensive and engaging learning experience.

Overall, this project will provide a holistic and integrated learning experience for students, giving them the opportunity to apply their knowledge and skills to real-world situations and contribute to building a sustainable future for our community.

The project can be assessed based on the following criteria:

- Creativity and Innovation in Garden Design
- Understanding of Different Plants and their Uses
- Knowledge of Sustainable Agriculture Practices
- Integration of Different Subjects in the Project
- Participation in Gardening Activities

Conclusion:

Through this project, students will not only learn about the importance of plants and sustainable agriculture practices but also develop an appreciation for nature and a sense of responsibility towards the environment. They will also learn how different subjects can be integrated to create a meaningful and engaging learning experience.

Skills and Competencies Enhanced:

Research and analysis skills: Students will be required to conduct research on different types of foods in India, including their history, geography, nutritional value, and cultural significance. They will also analyze data related to food production, consumption, and distribution.

Communication skills: Students will need to communicate their knowledge and experiences about different types of foods through various means such as writing, interviewing, creating digital presentations, and sharing their ideas with others.

Creative thinking and problem-solving skills: Students will be required to come up with innovative and sustainable solutions for promoting access to nutritious and culturally appropriate foods for all, and for promoting sustainable and equitable food systems.

Collaboration and teamwork skills: Students will work collaboratively with their peers, teachers, and community members to conduct research, plan and execute food tasting activities, and design food-related games and activities.

Cultural competency and empathy: Students will learn about the cultural and social significance of different types of foods in India, and will develop empathy for those who face food insecurity and inequitable access to healthy and culturally appropriate foods.

Health and wellness skills: Students will learn about the nutritional value and health benefits of different types of foods, and will participate in food-related sports activities to promote healthy eating and active lifestyles.

Information literacy and technology skills: Students will use various digital tools and platforms to conduct research, analyze data, create digital presentations and videos, and share their knowledge and experiences about different types of foods.

ppp

145

Project 2: Wild Adventures

Title: Wild Adventures/ Wild Wonders: Exploring the Wonders of Animal Life: Discover, Learn, and Protect!

Project Overview:

- In this project, the students will learn about the wonders of animal life, their habitats, behaviors, and the important roles they play in our ecosystem.
- They will explore different types of animals, their adaptations, and conservation efforts to protect them.
- They will also participate in a wildlife observation activity and learn about responsible animal tourism.

Subjects integrated:

Science, English, Social Studies, Value Education, Art, Sports, and Information Technology.

Learning outcomes:

Science:

- Students will be able to understand the basic characteristics and classifications of animals
- Students will be able to describe the adaptations and behaviors of different animals
- Students will be able to identify the importance of animal habitats and ecosystems

English:

- Students will be able to write descriptive paragraphs about different animals
- Students will be able to create brochures or posters to promote animal conservation
- Students will be able to write short stories or poems about animals

Social Studies:

- Students will be able to understand the importance of animal conservation and the impact of human activities on animal life
- Students will be able to understand the cultural significance of animals in different societies
- Students will be able to understand the role of zoos, sanctuaries, and wildlife reserves in animal conservation

Value Education:

- Students will be able to understand the importance of responsible animal tourism and ethical treatment of animals
- Students will be able to understand the importance of protecting endangered species and biodiversity

Art:

- Students will be able to create animal-themed art pieces using different mediums such as painting, drawing, and sculpture
- Students will be able to design posters or murals to promote animal conservation

Sports:

- Students will be able to participate in physical activities related to animal movements and behaviors
- Students will be able to understand the health benefits of outdoor activities and exploring nature

Information Technology:

- Students will be able to create digital presentations about different animals and their adaptations
- Students will be able to use technology to research and explore different animal habitats and behaviors

Assessment:

The project will be assessed based on creativity and innovation in animal conservation, understanding of different animals and their adaptations, knowledge of animal habitats and ecosystems, integration of different subjects in the project, and participation in wildlife observation and responsible animal tourism activities.

Final integrated outcome:

The final integrated outcome of the "Wild Adventures: Exploring the Wonders of Animal Life" project is a comprehensive understanding of the wonders of animal life, their importance in our ecosystem, and the need for responsible animal tourism and conservation efforts.

Through this project, students will have the opportunity to integrate different subjects and develop a deeper appreciation for nature and its wonders. They will learn about the characteristics and adaptations of different animals, the importance of animal habitats and ecosystems, and the cultural significance of animals in different societies. They will also develop an understanding of responsible animal tourism and ethical treatment of animals, and explore the possibilities of using art and technology for promoting animal conservation.

Overall, this project will provide a holistic and integrated learning experience for students, giving them the opportunity to apply their knowledge and skills to real-world situations and contribute to building a better future for our community and its wildlife.

Skills and Competencies Enhanced:

Research and analysis skills: Students will be required to conduct research on different types of animals, including their habitats, adaptations, behavior, and threats to their survival. They will also analyze data related to animal populations, distribution, and conservation.

Communication skills: Students will need to communicate their knowledge and experiences about animals through various means such as writing, drawing, creating digital presentations, and sharing their ideas with others.

Creative thinking and problem-solving skills: Students will be required to come up with innovative and sustainable solutions for protecting and conserving different types of animals and their habitats, and for promoting sustainable and equitable wildlife management practices.

Collaboration and teamwork skills: Students will work collaboratively with their peers, teachers, and community members to conduct research, plan and execute animal observation activities, and design animal-related games and activities.

Cultural competency and empathy: Students will learn about the cultural and social significance of different types of animals, and will develop empathy for those who face threats to their survival and well-being.

Environmental literacy and sustainability skills: Students will learn about the importance of preserving biodiversity and ecosystem services, and will participate in activities that promote sustainable and responsible use of natural resources.

Information literacy and technology skills: Students will use various digital tools and platforms to conduct research, analyze data, create digital presentations and videos, and share their knowledge and experiences about different types of animals.

ᗡᗡᗡ

146

Project 3: Climate Crusaders

Title: Climate Crusaders: Investigating Weather, Climate, and Seasons Understanding, Adapting, and Protecting!

Project Overview:

In this project, you will investigate weather patterns, climate zones, and seasonal changes, and explore the impact of climate change on our planet. You will learn about different types of weather phenomena, their causes and effects, and how to adapt to changing weather conditions. You will also participate in a weather observation activity and learn about actions we can take to protect our planet and achieve sustainable development.

Subjects integrated: Science, Math, English, Social Studies, Value Education, Art, and Information Technology.

SDG Goal: Goal 13: Climate Action

Learning outcomes:

Science:

- Students will be able to describe different types of weather phenomena, such as thunderstorms, hurricanes, and tornadoes
- Students will be able to explain the causes and effects of climate change on our planet
- Students will be able to understand the impact of human activities on the environment and climate

Math:

- Students will be able to interpret and analyze weather data, such as temperature, rainfall, and wind speed

- Students will be able to calculate and estimate the probability of different weather events

English:

- Students will be able to write descriptive paragraphs about different weather phenomena
- Students will be able to create brochures or posters to promote climate action and sustainability
- Students will be able to write short stories or poems about weather and seasons

Social Studies:

- Students will be able to understand the impact of climate change on different regions and communities
- Students will be able to understand the importance of international cooperation and action to address climate change
- Students will be able to understand the role of sustainable development in protecting our planet and ensuring a better future for all

Value Education:

- Students will be able to understand the importance of taking action to protect our planet and achieve sustainable development
- Students will be able to understand the impact of climate change on vulnerable communities and the importance of social and environmental justice
- Students will be able to understand the role of individual and collective action in promoting climate action and sustainability

Art:

- Students will be able to create weather-themed art pieces using different mediums such as painting, drawing, and sculpture
- Students will be able to design posters or murals to promote climate action and sustainability

Information Technology:

- Students will be able to create digital presentations about weather phenomena and climate change
- Students will be able to use technology to research and analyze weather data and its impact on our planet

Assessment:

The project will be assessed based on creativity and innovation in climate action, understanding of weather phenomena and climate change, knowledge of climate zones and seasonal changes, integration of different subjects in the project, and participation in weather observation and sustainability activities.

Final integrated outcome:

The final integrated outcome of the "Climate Crusaders: Investigating Weather, Climate, and Seasons" project is a comprehensive understanding of weather patterns, climate zones, and seasonal changes, and the need for climate action and sustainable development.

Through this project, students will have the opportunity to integrate different subjects and develop a deeper appreciation for our planet and its climate. They will learn about the causes and effects of climate change, the importance of international cooperation and action, and the role of sustainable development in protecting our planet and ensuring a better future for all. They will also develop an understanding of individual and collective action in promoting climate action and sustainability, and explore the possibilities of using art and technology for promoting climate action.

Overall, this project will provide a holistic and integrated learning experience for students, giving them the opportunity to apply their knowledge and skills to real-world situations and contribute to a sustainable future for all. The project will culminate in a climate action plan or a sustainability project, where students will demonstrate their understanding of climate change and propose actions to protect our planet and promote sustainable development. By the end of the project, students will have developed a deep understanding of weather, climate, and seasons, and their interconnections with human activities and sustainability. They will also have developed important skills such as critical thinking, problem-solving, collaboration, and communication, which are essential for their future success.

Skills and Competencies Enhanced:

Scientific inquiry and analysis skills: Students will use scientific methods to explore the concepts of weather, climate, and seasons, including data collection, analysis, and interpretation.

Communication skills: Students will need to communicate their knowledge and experiences about weather, climate, and seasons through various means such as writing, drawing, creating digital presentations, and sharing their ideas with others.

Critical thinking and problem-solving skills: Students will be required to analyze weather patterns and trends, predict weather changes, and develop strategies for adapting to changing weather and climate conditions.

Collaboration and teamwork skills: Students will work collaboratively with their peers, teachers, and community members to conduct research, plan and execute weather observation activities, and design weather-related games and activities.

Cultural competency and empathy: Students will learn about the cultural and social significance of weather and climate in different communities, and will develop empathy for those who face the impacts of climate change and extreme weather events.

Environmental literacy and sustainability skills: Students will learn about the impacts of climate change on the environment and human society, and will participate in activities that promote sustainable and responsible use of natural resources.

Information literacy and technology skills: Students will use various digital tools and platforms to conduct research, analyze data, create digital presentations and videos, and share their knowledge and experiences about weather, climate, and seasons.

ppp

147

Project 4: Foodies Unite

Title: Foodies Unite: Exploring Different Types of Foods in India
Savor, Discover, and Play!
Project Overview:

In this project, you will explore the rich diversity of foods in India, and learn about the cultural, social, and economic aspects of food production and consumption. You will investigate the history and geography of different types of foods, and their nutritional value and health benefits. You will also participate in a food-tasting activity and learn about the importance of sports and physical activities in maintaining a healthy and balanced lifestyle.

Subjects integrated:

Science, Math, English, Hindi, Social Studies, Value Education, Art, Information Technology, and Sports.

SDG Goal: Goal 2: Zero Hunger
Learning outcomes:
Science:

- Students will be able to understand the nutritional value and health benefits of different types of foods
- Students will be able to understand the science behind food production and preservation
- Students will be able to identify different types of crops and their growing conditions

Math:

- Students will be able to analyze data related to food production, consumption, and distribution
- Students will be able to calculate the nutritional content of different foods
- Students will be able to estimate the cost of producing and consuming different types of foods

English/Hindi:

- Students will be able to write descriptive paragraphs about different types of foods and their cultural significance
- Students will be able to create recipes and food blogs to share their knowledge and experiences
- Students will be able to conduct interviews with local farmers and food vendors to learn about their livelihoods and challenges

Social Studies:

- Students will be able to understand the history and geography of different types of foods in India
- Students will be able to understand the cultural and social significance of food in different regions and communities
- Students will be able to understand the impact of food production and consumption on the environment and sustainability

Value Education:

- Students will be able to understand the importance of access to nutritious and culturally appropriate foods for all
- Students will be able to understand the importance of sustainable and equitable food systems for achieving zero hunger
- Students will be able to understand the role of individual and collective action in promoting food security and sustainable agriculture

Art:

- Students will be able to create food-themed art pieces using different mediums such as painting, drawing, and collage

- Students will be able to design food packaging and advertising materials
- Students will be able to create food-related games and activities for promoting healthy eating and active lifestyles

Information Technology:

- Students will be able to create digital presentations and videos about different types of foods and their nutritional value
- Students will be able to use technology to research and analyze data related to food production and consumption
- Students will be able to create online platforms for sharing their knowledge and experiences about different types of foods

Sports:

- Students will be able to understand the importance of sports and physical activities in maintaining a healthy and balanced lifestyle
- Students will be able to learn about the nutritional needs of athletes and how different types of foods can support their performance
- Students will be able to participate in food-related sports activities, such as cooking competitions and taste-testing games

Assessment:
The project will be assessed based on creativity and innovation in promoting sustainable and equitable food systems, understanding of different types of foods and their nutritional value, integration of different subjects in the project, and participation in food tasting and sports activities.

Final integrated outcome:
The final outcome of the "Foodies Unite: Exploring Different Types of Foods in India" project can be a presentation or a report that showcases the knowledge gained and experiences during the project. The presentation or report can have the following sections:

Introduction: Provide a brief overview of the project and its objectives. Also, introduce the SDG Goal 2: Zero Hunger and how the project is aligned with it.

History and Geography of Indian Cuisine: Explore the history of Indian cuisine and its different influences. Investigate the geographical regions of India and their culinary specialties.

Nutritional Value and Health Benefits: Research the nutritional value and health benefits of different Indian foods. Discuss how the traditional Indian diet can contribute to a healthy and balanced lifestyle.

Food Tasting Activity: Share the experience of the food tasting activity and highlight the different types of Indian foods tasted. Include pictures and descriptions of the dishes.

Cultural and Social Aspects of Food: Explore the cultural and social aspects of food production and consumption in India. Discuss how food is an integral part of Indian festivals and celebrations.

Importance of Sports and Physical Activities: Explain the importance of sports and physical activities in maintaining a healthy lifestyle. Share the experiences of participating in sports activities during the project.

Conclusion: Summarize the key takeaways from the project, including the knowledge gained, experiences, and how the project aligns with SDG Goal 2: Zero Hunger.

References: Include a list of references used during the project.

The final outcome can be presented in various formats, such as a PowerPoint presentation, a poster, or a written report. It can also include multimedia elements such as pictures, videos, and audio recordings.

Skills and Competencies Enhanced:

Research and analysis skills: Students will be required to conduct research on different types of foods in India, including their history, geography, nutritional value, and cultural significance. They will also analyze data related to food production, consumption, and distribution.

Communication skills: Students will need to communicate their knowledge and experiences about different types of foods through various means such as writing, interviewing, creating digital presentations, and sharing their ideas with others.

Creative thinking and problem-solving skills: Students will be required to come up with innovative and sustainable solutions for promoting access to nutritious and culturally appropriate foods for all, and for promoting sustainable and equitable food systems.

Collaboration and teamwork skills: Students will work collaboratively with their peers, teachers, and community members to conduct research, plan and execute food tasting activities, and design food-related games and activities.

Cultural competency and empathy: Students will learn about the cultural and social significance of different types of foods in India, and will develop empathy for those who face food insecurity and inequitable access to healthy and culturally appropriate foods.

Health and wellness skills: Students will learn about the nutritional value and health benefits of different types of foods, and will participate in food-related sports activities to promote healthy eating and active lifestyles.

Information literacy and technology skills: Students will use various digital tools and platforms to conduct research, analyze data, create digital presentations and videos, and share their knowledge and experiences about different types of foods.

ᐅᐅᐅ

148

Project 5: Birds of India

Title: "Birds of India: Exploring Avian Diversity Across States"
"Fly High with Knowledge, Protect the Feathered Friends!"
Project Overview:

In this project, you will explore the diverse avian species found across different Indian states. You will learn about their physical features, habitats, diet, and behavior. You will also investigate their cultural and mythological significance, and the conservation efforts aimed at protecting them.

Subjects integrated:

Science, Math, English, Hindi, Social Studies, Value Education, Information Technology, and Sports.

SDG Goal: Goal 15: Life on Land

Learning Outcomes

Science:

- Students will learn about the physical features, habitats, diet, and behavior of different avian species found in India.
- Students will develop an understanding of the anatomy and physiology of birds and how it relates to their habitats and lifestyle.
- Students will learn about the conservation efforts aimed at protecting different bird species and their habitats.

Math:

- Students can collect data on different bird species observed during bird-watching and photography activities and create tables, graphs, and charts to analyze and interpret the data.

English:

- Students will develop reading, writing, and speaking skills through researching and presenting their findings about different bird species.
- Students can read and analyze literature about birds and their cultural and mythological significance in different Indian states.

Hindi:

- Students can explore the cultural and mythological significance of birds in different Indian states through reading and analyzing Hindi literature about birds.

Social Studies:

- Students will learn about the diversity of avian species found in different Indian states and how it relates to the cultural and environmental diversity of India.
- Students can investigate the traditional knowledge and practices related to avian biodiversity in different Indian communities.

Value Education:

- Students will develop an appreciation for the value of biodiversity and the importance of conserving it for future generations.
- Students can learn about the ethical considerations related to the use and conservation of birds and their habitats.

Information Technology:

- Students can use digital tools and online resources to research and document different bird species and their habitats.

Sports:

- Students will learn about the importance of physical activities in maintaining a healthy and balanced lifestyle and how it relates to bird-watching and other outdoor activities.

Overall, this project provides a unique opportunity for students to develop interdisciplinary learning outcomes in a variety of subjects, as well as important competencies and skills.

Project Steps:

- Introduction: Provide an overview of the project and its objectives. Introduce the SDG Goal 15: Life on Land and how the project aligns with it.
- Types of Birds: Research and identify different types of birds found in different Indian states. Categorize them based on their physical features and habitats.
- Avian Anatomy and Physiology: Explore the anatomy and physiology of birds. Discuss how their physical features are adapted to their habitats and lifestyle.
- Bird-watching and Photography: Engage in bird-watching and photography activities to observe and document different bird species. Learn about the different tools and techniques used in bird-watching and photography.
- Cultural and Mythological Significance: Investigate the cultural and mythological significance of birds in different Indian states. Discuss how birds are represented in art, literature, and mythology.
- Conservation Efforts: Learn about the conservation efforts aimed at protecting different bird species and their habitats. Discuss the importance of biodiversity and the role of humans in conserving it.
- Conclusion: Summarize the key takeaways from the project, including the knowledge gained, experiences, and how the project aligns with SDG Goal 15: Life on Land.
- References: Include a list of references used during the project.

Final Outcome:

The final outcome of the project can be a presentation, a report, or a poster showcasing the knowledge gained and experiences during the project. The presentation or report can include multimedia elements such as pictures, videos, and audio recordings.

Skills and Competencies Enhanced:

Scientific Inquiry Skills: The project involves researching and identifying different types of birds found in different Indian states. Students will learn to use scientific inquiry skills such as observing, questioning, and investigating to gain knowledge about avian species.

Data Analysis and Interpretation: Students will collect and document data on different bird species observed during bird-watching and photography activities. They will learn how to analyze and interpret data to draw conclusions about avian diversity in India.

Communication Skills: The project requires students to present their findings through presentations, reports, or posters. They will develop communication skills such as public speaking, writing, and visual presentation to effectively convey their knowledge and experiences.

Cultural Awareness and Appreciation: Students will learn about the cultural and mythological significance of birds in different Indian states. They will develop an appreciation for the cultural diversity in India and how it relates to biodiversity.

Critical Thinking and Problem Solving: The project involves investigating the conservation efforts aimed at protecting different bird species and their habitats. Students will learn how to think critically and develop problem-solving skills to address the challenges facing avian biodiversity in India.

Technology Skills: The project involves using technology such as cameras and online resources to document and research different bird species. Students will develop technology skills such as using digital tools and online platforms to support their learning.

Teamwork and Collaboration: Students can work in teams to conduct bird-watching and photography activities and to present their findings. They will develop teamwork and collaboration skills such as listening, contributing ideas, and supporting each other.

Assessment Rubrics:

Criteria | Excellent | Good | Fair | Needs Improvement |

Scientific Inquiry Skills:

Demonstrates scientific inquiry skills | 4 | 3 | 2 | 1

Data Analysis and Interpretation:

Analyzes and interprets data | 4 | 3 | 2 | 1

Communication Skills:

Communicates findings effectively | 4 | 3 | 2 | 1

Cultural Awareness and Appreciation:

Demonstrates cultural awareness and appreciation | 4 | 3 | 2 | 1

Critical Thinking and Problem-Solving:

Demonstrates critical thinking and problem-solving skills | 4 | 3 | 2 | 1

Technology Skills:
Demonstrates technology skills | 4 | 3 | 2 | 1
Teamwork and Collaboration:
Works collaboratively in a team | 4 | 3 | 2 | 1
SDG Goal:
Demonstrates understanding of SDG Goal 15: Life on Land | 4 | 3 | 2 | 1
Overall Performance:
Overall performance in the project | 4 | 3 | 2 | 1

Exceeds Expectations: Demonstrates exceptional understanding and application of the competencies and skills listed.

Meets Expectations: Demonstrates adequate understanding and application of the competencies and skills listed.

Partially Meets Expectations: Demonstrates some understanding and application of the competencies and skills listed.

Does Not Meet Expectations: Demonstrates limited understanding and application of the competencies and skills listed.

This rubric assesses student performance based on various competencies and skills listed in the project description. Each criterion is assigned a rating from 1 to 4, with 4 being the highest score. The rubric also includes a description of what constitutes an excellent, good, fair, or needs improvement performance in each criterion. Finally, an overall performance score is assigned based on the student's overall understanding and application of the competencies and skills.

ϸϸϸ

149

Project 6: Threads of Diversity

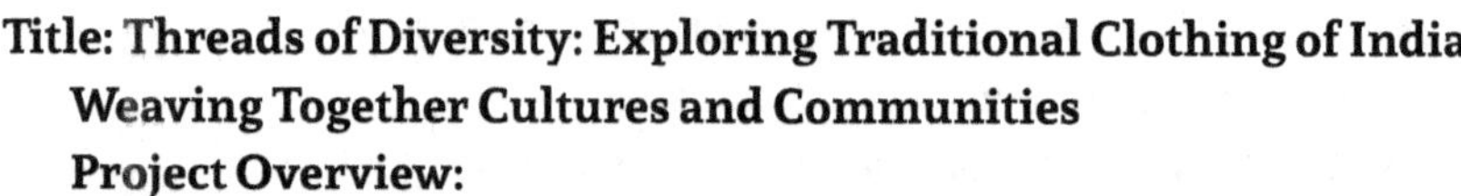

Title: Threads of Diversity: Exploring Traditional Clothing of India Weaving Together Cultures and Communities

Project Overview:

In this project, you will explore the rich diversity of traditional clothing worn by people in different states of India. You will learn about the history, culture, and significance of clothing in different regions, and investigate the materials and techniques used in their production. You will also develop empathy by considering how clothing choices reflect people's identities, lifestyles, and values, and how they may be influenced by social, economic, and environmental factors. Finally, you will use your research findings to create a digital presentation showcasing the beauty and diversity of Indian clothing.

Subjects integrated:

Science (Textiles and Fibers), Math (Measurement and Patterns), English (Research and Communication Skills), Hindi (Regional Languages), Social Studies (Cultural Diversity and Identity), Value Education (Empathy and Respect), Information Technology (Digital Presentation), and Sports (Physical Fitness and Comfortable Clothing).

SDG Goal: Goal 10: Reduced Inequalities and Goal 12: Responsible Consumption and Production

Learning Outcomes:

Science:

- Students will be able to identify the materials used in the production of traditional clothing in different states of India.

- Students will be able to explain how natural resources are used in the production of different types of clothing.
- Students will be able to understand the environmental impact of clothing production and consumption.

Math:

- Students will be able to analyze data on different types of clothing worn in different states of India.
- Students will be able to create charts and graphs to visually represent patterns in clothing choices.
- Students will be able to calculate the cost of producing different types of clothing.

English:

- Students will be able to write detailed notes and explanations of the different types of clothing worn in different states of India.
- Students will be able to present their research findings in a clear and organized manner.
- Students will be able to communicate effectively with their peers and teachers during the project.

Hindi:

- Students will be able to identify and understand Hindi terms related to different types of clothing in different states of India.
- Students will be able to use Hindi language skills to communicate effectively with their peers and teachers during the project.
- Students will be able to understand the cultural significance of Hindi language in Indian society.

Social Studies:

- Students will be able to understand the cultural diversity of different states of India through the clothing worn by people in each region.
- Students will be able to identify the social and economic factors that influence clothing choices in different regions of India.

- Students will be able to appreciate the beauty and uniqueness of different traditional clothing styles in India.

Value Education:

- Students will be able to understand the importance of respecting and appreciating cultural diversity.
- Students will be able to empathize with people from different regions of India and understand how their clothing choices reflect their identities, values, and lifestyles.
- Students will be able to develop a sense of curiosity and appreciation for different cultures and traditions.

Information Technology:

- Students will be able to use digital tools and platforms to research, collect, and analyze data on traditional clothing in different states of India.
- Students will be able to create a digital presentation to showcase their research findings.
- Students will be able to develop skills in digital literacy, including online research, data analysis, and presentation design.

Sports:

- Students will be able to understand the importance of clothing choices in different sports and physical activities.
- Students will be able to appreciate the significance of clothing in maintaining comfort, safety, and performance during physical activities.
- Students will be able to develop an understanding of the cultural and regional differences in sports and physical activities in India.

SDG Goal:
Goal 10: Reduced Inequalities - Through understanding and appreciating the diversity of clothing choices in different regions of India, students can develop a sense of empathy and respect for different cultures and traditions, and work towards reducing inequalities based on cultural differences.
Key Competencies and Skills Enhanced:

- Scientific inquiry skills
- Research and communication skills
- Cultural awareness and appreciation
- Empathy and respect
- Digital literacy
- Physical fitness and comfort

Rubric Criteria:

- Scientific Inquiry Skills
- Research and Communication Skills
- Cultural Awareness and Appreciation
- Empathy and Respect
- Digital Literacy
- Physical Fitness and Comfort
- Overall Performance

Exceeds Expectations: Demonstrates exceptional understanding and application of the competencies and skills listed.

Meets Expectations: Demonstrates adequate understanding and application of the competencies and skills listed.

Partially Meets Expectations: Demonstrates some understanding and application of the competencies and skills listed.

Does Not Meet Expectations: Demonstrates limited understanding and application of the competencies and skills listed.

Project Format

Research: Conduct research on traditional clothing worn by people in different states of India. You should explore the history, culture, significance, materials, and techniques used in the production of these clothes.

Data Collection: Collect data on the clothing you have researched. You should take pictures of different types of clothes and write detailed notes about each piece of clothing.

Analysis: Analyze the data you have collected and look for patterns in the types of clothing worn in different states. You should also consider the cultural, social, and economic factors that influence the clothing choices of people in these states.

Presentation: Use the data you have collected and analyzed to create a digital presentation showcasing the beauty and diversity of Indian clothing. Your presentation should include pictures, notes, and explanations of the different types of clothes worn in each state, as well as the cultural, social, and economic factors that influence clothing choices. You should also include your own reflections on what you have learned about the significance of clothing in different regions of India.

The final project should be a digital presentation that demonstrates your research, analysis, and reflection on traditional clothing worn by people in different states of India. The presentation should be visually engaging and include detailed explanations and notes to help your audience understand the significance and beauty of Indian clothing. Make sure your presentation is well-organized, and informative, and reflects your creativity and passion for learning about the cultural diversity of India.

Remember to also incorporate empathy into your research by considering how clothing choices reflect people's identities, lifestyles, and values, and how they may be influenced by social, economic, and environmental factors.

Skills and Competencies Enhanced (in detail)

Research skills - Students will develop skills in conducting research, collecting and analyzing data, and synthesizing information from different sources.

Communication skills - Students will develop skills in communicating their research findings effectively, through written and oral presentations.

Cultural awareness - Students will develop an understanding of the cultural diversity of India, and appreciate the significance of traditional clothing styles in different regions.

Empathy - Students will develop empathy towards people from different regions of India, and understand how their clothing choices reflect their identities, values, and lifestyles.

Critical thinking - Students will develop skills in analyzing and interpreting data, identifying patterns and trends, and drawing conclusions from their research findings.

Creative thinking - Students will have the opportunity to develop their creativity, by designing and creating their own traditional clothing styles.

Digital literacy - Students will develop skills in using digital tools and platforms to conduct research, analyze data, and create digital presentations.

Teamwork - Students will work in teams to conduct their research and present their findings, developing skills in collaboration and cooperation.

Time management - Students will learn to manage their time effectively, setting deadlines for their research tasks and completing them in a timely manner.

Problem-solving - Students may encounter challenges or obstacles during the project, and will develop skills in problem-solving and finding creative solutions.

Respect for diversity - Through understanding and appreciating the diversity of clothing choices in different regions of India, students will develop a sense of respect for different cultures and traditions.

Environmental awareness - Students will learn about the environmental impact of clothing production and consumption, and develop an awareness of the need to reduce waste and conserve natural resources.

ppp

150
Eliciting Evidence of Learning

Here are some ways to elicit evidence of learning in primary school students for the science subject:

Science Projects: Assign students with hands-on projects to demonstrate their understanding of scientific concepts. Projects can include designing and conducting experiments, building models, creating displays, or conducting research.

Science Journals: Ask students to keep a journal to document their scientific observations and discoveries. They can record their findings, draw pictures, and write explanations of what they observed.

Science Reports: Assign students to write reports on various scientific topics, such as plants, animals, or the human body. This will not only test their understanding of the subject matter but also their writing skills.

Science Quizzes: Conduct quizzes to test students' understanding of scientific concepts. These quizzes can be oral or written and can be conducted as group or individual activities.

Science Presentations: Assign students to make presentations to the class on scientific topics. This can be in the form of PowerPoint presentations, posters, or verbal presentations.

ϸϸϸ

Science Experiments: Conduct experiments in the classroom to assess students' understanding of scientific concepts. You can observe how they perform the experiment and how they interpret the results.

ϸϸϸ

Science Games: Engage students in fun, interactive games that help them learn scientific concepts. Games can include online quizzes, puzzles, or board games.

ϸϸϸ

Science Observations: Ask students to observe their surroundings and report on what they see. This can help develop their observational skills and provide insight into their understanding of scientific concepts.

ϸϸϸ

Science Graphic Organizers: Provide students with graphic organizers, such as concept maps or Venn diagrams, to help them organize their understanding of scientific concepts. This will not only help them to retain the information but also provide evidence of their understanding.

ϸϸϸ

Science Reflections: Ask students to reflect on what they have learned in science class. Reflections can be written or verbal and can help students to develop a deeper understanding of the concepts they are learning.

ϸϸϸ

Science Interviews: Conduct interviews with students to assess their understanding of scientific concepts. You can ask them questions related to the topic and observe how they respond.

ϸϸϸ

Science Debates: Assign students to debate scientific topics in class. This can help them to develop critical thinking and communication skills while also demonstrating their understanding of the topic.

ϸϸϸ

Science Collaborations: Assign students to work collaboratively on science projects or experiments. This will not only help them to develop teamwork skills but also provide evidence of their understanding of the scientific concepts being taught.

ᗞᗞᗞ

By using a variety of assessment methods, you can elicit evidence of learning in primary school students for the science subject and ensure that they have a comprehensive understanding of the concepts they are learning.

151

Activating Students' Prior Knowledge

Here are some ways to activate primary students' prior knowledge during science class:

KWL Charts: Use KWL (Know, Want to Know, Learned) charts to activate students' prior knowledge. Begin by asking students what they already know about the topic, what they want to know, and what they hope to learn. This helps to identify any misconceptions or gaps in their knowledge, while also stimulating their curiosity.

❧❧❧

Concept Mapping: Use concept mapping to help students connect prior knowledge to new information. Ask students to draw a map of what they know about a topic, including related concepts and relationships between them. This helps them to visualize the connections and better understand the new information.

❧❧❧

Pre-Assessments: Administer a pre-assessment before introducing new material. This helps to identify students' prior knowledge and misconceptions, which can then be addressed during the lesson.

❧❧❧

Think-Pair-Share: Use the think-pair-share strategy to activate prior knowledge. Ask students to think about a topic, pair up with a partner, and share their ideas. This encourages students to discuss their prior knowledge and develop a deeper understanding of the topic.

ᗌᗌᗌ

Inquiry-Based Learning: Use inquiry-based learning to activate prior knowledge. Ask students to investigate a topic, conduct experiments, and draw conclusions. This helps them to connect prior knowledge to new information and develop critical thinking skills.

ᗌᗌᗌ

Review Games: Use review games to activate prior knowledge. Divide students into teams and ask questions related to prior learning. This helps to reinforce prior knowledge and provides an opportunity for students to engage in friendly competition.

ᗌᗌᗌ

Hands-on Activities: Use hands-on activities to activate prior knowledge. For example, ask students to bring in objects related to the topic, or conduct a simple experiment that connects prior knowledge to new information. This helps to engage students and provide a concrete connection between prior knowledge and new concepts.

ᗌᗌᗌ

Brainstorming: Use brainstorming to activate prior knowledge. Ask students to brainstorm everything they know about a topic, and write their ideas on a whiteboard or flip chart. This helps to generate ideas and stimulate discussion.

ᗌᗌᗌ

Anchoring Phenomena: Use anchoring phenomena to activate prior knowledge. Anchoring phenomena are real-world examples that connect to the topic and engage students in scientific thinking. For example, if you're teaching about plant growth, you might use a video or picture of a plant growing in different conditions to spark discussion and activate prior knowledge.

ᗌᗌᗌ

Graphic Organizers: Use graphic organizers, such as mind maps, Venn diagrams, or concept maps, to activate prior knowledge. These organizers help students to organize their thoughts and identify connections between concepts.

ϷϷϷ

Concept Attainment: Use concept attainment to activate prior knowledge. This strategy involves presenting examples and non-examples of a concept and asking students to identify the concept. This helps to activate prior knowledge and clarify misconceptions.

ϷϷϷ

Digital Tools: Use digital tools to activate prior knowledge. For example, you can use online quizzes or games to assess students' prior knowledge or create interactive lessons that engage students in scientific thinking. Digital tools can be particularly engaging for students and help to make connections between prior knowledge and new information.

ϷϷϷ

152

Activating Learners as Owners of their Learning

Here are some strategies for activating primary school students as owners of their own learning:

Student-Led Conferences: Hold student-led conferences in which students share their learning with their families. Students can showcase their work and discuss their learning goals, progress, and achievements. This helps students take ownership of their learning and empowers them to share their successes and challenges with others.

❧❧❧

Self-Assessment: Encourage students to self-assess their learning progress. Provide them with clear criteria and rubrics, and ask them to evaluate their work against these criteria. This helps students to take ownership of their learning, identify areas for improvement, and set goals for themselves.

❧❧❧

Choice-Based Learning: Allow students to choose what they learn, how they learn, and how they demonstrate their learning. This helps students to take ownership of their learning and make meaningful connections to their own lives.

❧❧❧

Student Goal-Setting: Encourage students to set their own learning goals, both short-term and long-term. This helps students to take ownership of their learning, develop self-awareness, and take responsibility for their progress.

ÞÞÞ

Inquiry-Based Learning: Use inquiry-based learning to empower students to take ownership of their learning. This approach involves asking students to investigate questions and problems that interest them, and to develop their own understanding of the concepts being studied.

ÞÞÞ

Student Reflection: Encourage students to reflect on their learning regularly. This can be done through journaling, group discussions, or other reflection activities. Reflection helps students to take ownership of their learning, make connections between concepts, and identify areas for improvement.

ÞÞÞ

Collaborative Learning: Encourage students to work collaboratively on learning projects or assignments. This helps students to take ownership of their learning, develop teamwork skills, and learn from each other.

ÞÞÞ

Student-Led Learning Activities: Encourage students to lead their own learning activities, such as presentations, debates, or class discussions. This helps students to take ownership of their learning and develop leadership and communication skills.

ÞÞÞ

Reflection-Based Assessments: Use reflection-based assessments, such as self-evaluations, peer evaluations, or feedback sessions, to empower students to take ownership of their learning. These assessments help students to reflect on their own learning progress and identify areas for improvement.

ÞÞÞ

Personalized Learning: Tailor learning experiences to the unique needs and interests of each student. This helps students to take ownership of their learning and feel more engaged and motivated.

ÞÞÞ

Problem-Based Learning: Use problem-based learning to empower students to take ownership of their learning. This approach involves presenting students with a real-world problem or scenario and asking them to work collaboratively to develop a solution. This helps students to develop critical thinking and problem-solving skills, while also taking ownership of their learning.

ᐅᐅᐅ

Student Portfolios: Use student portfolios to empower students to take ownership of their learning. Portfolios allow students to showcase their best work and track their learning progress over time. This helps students to take ownership of their learning, identify areas for improvement, and set goals for themselves.

ᐅᐅᐅ

By using these strategies, you can help activate primary school students as owners of their own learning, leading to increased engagement, motivation, and academic success.

153
The Feedback that Moves Learning Forward

"Empowering learners with feedback that inspires progress!"

Specific Feedback: "You did a great job with your experiment! Your hypothesis was clear and your methodology was well thought out. However, your data table needs more detail. Make sure to include all the relevant information in your future experiments."

ᐅᐅᐅ

Future-Focused Feedback: "Your drawing of the plant cell is great! To take it to the next level, try labeling the different parts of the cell and adding a brief description of their functions."

ᚦᚦᚦ

Feedback on Process: "I noticed that you spent a lot of time carefully observing the insects in the field. This is a great way to gather data for your research. Keep up the good work!"

ᚦᚦᚦ

Feedback on Effort: "I can see that you put a lot of effort into your science project. Although there is room for improvement, I appreciate the hard work that you put in. Let's work together to make it even better."

ᚦᚦᚦ

Feedback on Strengths: "Your explanation of the water cycle was very clear and easy to understand. You have a real talent for explaining scientific concepts. Keep up the good work!"

ᚦᚦᚦ

Feedback on Areas for Improvement: "Your science experiment was interesting, but you could improve it by making sure to follow the steps carefully and recording your data accurately. Let's work together to make your next experiment even better."

ᚦᚦᚦ

Actionable Feedback: "To improve your understanding of the scientific method, I suggest practicing by conducting more experiments and recording your observations carefully. Here are some resources to help you get started."

ᚦᚦᚦ

Peer Feedback: "Great job on your presentation! Your experiment was very creative and you explained it very well. One suggestion I have is to speak a little slower so that the audience can follow along better."

ᚦᚦᚦ

Self-Reflection Feedback: "I thought my science project went well, but I could have spent more time practicing my presentation. Next time, I'll make sure to practice more beforehand."

ppp

Goal-Oriented Feedback: "Your science experiment was a great start! Let's work together to set some goals for your next experiment and plan out the steps you'll need to take to achieve them."

ppp

Specific Feedback: "Your lab report was well-written and organized. You provided detailed descriptions of the procedures and results, but you could have added more analysis and conclusions based on your findings. Keep up the good work!"

ppp

Future-Focused Feedback: "You did a great job identifying different animal tracks during our nature walk! Next time, try to take pictures of the tracks and see if you can identify the animal based on the shape and size of the tracks."

ppp

Feedback on Process: "I noticed that you spent a lot of time asking questions and making observations during our field trip. This is a great way to learn more about the environment and ecosystems. Keep it up!"

ppp

Feedback on Effort: "I can see that you put a lot of effort into your science project. Although there is room for improvement, I appreciate the hard work that you put in. Let's work together to make it even better."

ppp

Feedback on Strengths: "Your model of the solar system was very creative and detailed. You have a great eye for detail and a strong understanding of scientific concepts. Keep up the good work!"

ppp

Feedback on Areas for Improvement: "Your experiment was interesting, but you could improve it by controlling variables more carefully and conducting multiple trials. Let's work together to make your next experiment even better."

ᚦᚦᚦ

Actionable Feedback: "To improve your understanding of the human body, I suggest practicing by identifying different organs and their functions. Here are some resources to help you get started."

ᚦᚦᚦ

Peer Feedback: "Great job on your project! Your presentation was engaging and you provided a lot of interesting facts about the environment. One suggestion I have is to add more visuals to help the audience follow along."

ᚦᚦᚦ

Self-Reflection Feedback: "I thought my experiment went well, but I could have prepared better by organizing my materials more carefully. Next time, I'll make sure to plan ahead more thoroughly."

ᚦᚦᚦ

Goal-Oriented Feedback: "Your science project was great! Let's work together to set some goals for your next project and come up with a plan to achieve them."

ᚦᚦᚦ

154

Learning Intentions

Learning Intentions guide the way!

"Know what you'll learn before you learn it - Learning Intentions guide the way!"

Learning Intentions are clear and specific statements that describe what students are expected to know, understand, and be able to do by the end of a lesson or unit. They help to guide instruction and provide a roadmap for learning.

Here are some examples of learning intentions for primary school science students according to Bloom's Taxonomy:

- **Remembering:** To recall scientific facts, concepts, and vocabulary, such as the names of different planets, the parts of a plant, or the characteristics of different states of matter.
- **Understanding:** To demonstrate comprehension of scientific ideas and principles, such as the laws of motion, the water cycle, or the food chain.
- **Applying:** To apply scientific knowledge and concepts to real-world situations, such as using the scientific method to investigate a problem or designing an experiment to test a hypothesis.
- **Analyzing:** To analyze scientific data and information, such as identifying patterns in a set of data or evaluating the credibility of a scientific claim.
- **Evaluating:** To evaluate the strengths and weaknesses of scientific arguments and evidence, such as comparing and contrasting different theories or assessing the reliability of a scientific source.
- **Creating:** To create new scientific knowledge and ideas, such as designing a new invention or developing a new theory to explain a natural phenomenon.

It is important to note that these learning intentions can be modified and adapted based on the specific needs and abilities of each student. Additionally, it is important to include a variety of learning experiences and assessment methods to ensure that students are engaging with the material at all levels of Bloom's Taxonomy.

ᐅᐅᐅ

Here are some examples of learning intentions for primary school science students according to multiple intelligences:

- **Verbal-linguistic:** To develop scientific language and communication skills, such as explaining scientific concepts in written or oral presentations, writing lab reports, or participating in class discussions.

- **Logical-mathematical:** To develop problem-solving and analytical skills in science, such as using data to make predictions, designing experiments, or creating models to explain natural phenomena.
- **Visual-spatial:** To develop visual and spatial skills in science, such as using diagrams, maps, and models to represent scientific ideas, or creating visual displays of scientific data.
- **Bodily-kinesthetic:** To develop hands-on and experiential learning in science, such as conducting experiments, doing fieldwork, or building and testing prototypes.
- **Musical:** To develop the use of music and sound in science learning, such as creating musical compositions to explain scientific concepts or using sound to explore scientific phenomena.
- **Interpersonal:** To develop collaborative and social skills in science learning, such as working in groups to conduct experiments or participating in class discussions and debates.
- **Intrapersonal:** To develop self-reflection and self-evaluation skills in science learning, such as setting goals, monitoring progress, and reflecting on personal learning experiences.
- **Naturalistic:** To develop an appreciation for the natural world and its systems, such as studying ecosystems, identifying plant and animal species, or exploring natural resources and conservation.

It is important to note that these learning intentions can be modified and adapted based on the specific needs and abilities of each student. Additionally, it is important to include a variety of learning experiences and assessment methods to ensure that students are engaging with the material in a way that is meaningful and engaging for them.

ᐳᐳᐳ

Here are some examples of learning intentions for primary school science students related to each of the 17 Sustainable Development Goals (SDGs):

SDG 1 - No poverty: To develop an understanding of the impacts of poverty on health, including access to safe water and sanitation, and ways to address poverty through sustainable development.

SDG 2 - Zero hunger: To develop an understanding of sustainable agriculture and food production, including the role of biodiversity in food security and ways to reduce food waste.

SDG 3 - Good health and well-being: To develop an understanding of human biology and health, such as learning about the body's systems, healthy habits, and preventing and treating common diseases.

SDG 4 - Quality education: To develop scientific inquiry and critical thinking skills, such as using the scientific method to investigate questions, evaluating scientific claims, and analyzing data.

SDG 5 - Gender equality: To develop an understanding of gender and its impacts on health, education, and development, including ways to promote gender equality in STEM fields.

SDG 6 - Clean water and sanitation: To develop an understanding of water and its properties, the importance of access to clean water, and how to conserve water resources.

SDG 7 - Affordable and clean energy: To develop an understanding of renewable and non-renewable energy sources, the benefits and drawbacks of each, and ways to reduce energy consumption.

SDG 8 - Decent work and economic growth: To develop an understanding of sustainable economic development, including the impact of economic growth on the environment and ways to promote sustainable business practices.

SDG 9 - Industry, innovation, and infrastructure: To develop an understanding of sustainable infrastructure and technology, including ways to promote innovation and reduce environmental impact.

SDG 10 - Reduced inequalities: To develop an understanding of the impacts of inequality on health, education, and development, including ways to promote social justice and equality.

SDG 11 - Sustainable cities and communities: To develop an understanding of sustainable urban development, including the impact of urbanization on the environment and ways to promote sustainable living.

SDG 12 - Responsible consumption and production: To develop an understanding of environmental sustainability, the impacts of human activity on natural resources, and ways to reduce waste and consumption.

SDG 13 - Climate action: To develop an understanding of climate change and its causes, the impact of human activity on the environment, and ways to reduce carbon emissions.

SDG 14 - Life below water: To develop an understanding of marine ecosystems and biodiversity, threats to ocean health, and ways to protect and conserve marine life.

SDG 15 - Life on land: To develop an understanding of terrestrial ecosystems and biodiversity, threats to land health, and ways to protect and conserve land-based life.

SDG 16 - Peace, justice, and strong institutions: To develop an understanding of human rights and social justice, including ways to promote peace and justice in local and global communities.

SDG 17 - Partnerships for the goals: To develop an understanding of international cooperation and partnership, including ways to promote sustainable development through global partnerships.

It is important to note that these learning intentions can be modified and adapted based on the specific needs and abilities of each student. Additionally, it is important to include a variety of learning experiences and assessment methods to ensure that students are engaging with the material in a way that is meaningful and engaging for them, while also helping to achieve the SDGs.

ᐅᐅᐅ

155

Learning Ladder

Scaling new heights in education

"Scaling new heights in education!"-Unlock your potential, one step at a time with Learning Ladder!

In the context of the Revised Bloom's Taxonomy, a Learning Ladder is a visual tool that outlines a sequence of increasingly complex cognitive tasks or levels of thinking for a specific topic or subject area. The Learning Ladder provides a roadmap for teachers and students to follow as they progress through a lesson or unit of study, and it helps to ensure that learning objectives are being met at each level of cognitive complexity.

Each rung of the Learning Ladder represents a different level of thinking, and these levels are based on the six cognitive processes outlined in the

Revised Bloom's Taxonomy:

- Remembering: recalling previously learned information
- Understanding: comprehending the meaning of information
- Applying: using the information in a new situation
- Analyzing: breaking down information into parts and examining relationships among them
- Evaluating: making judgments about the value or quality of information
- Creating: putting together different elements to form a new and original whole

As students move up the Learning Ladder, they are expected to engage in increasingly complex thinking tasks, building on the knowledge and skills they have acquired at each level. The Learning Ladder helps to ensure that students are challenged appropriately and are given opportunities to develop their thinking skills to the fullest extent.

Topic: States of Matter

- Level 1 - Remembering: Recall the three states of matter and the characteristics of each state.
- Level 2 - Understanding: Explain the behavior of particles in each state of matter and identify examples of each state in everyday life.
- Level 3 - Applying: Demonstrate how to change the state of matter of a substance by applying heat or cold and explain the scientific principles behind the changes.
- Level 4 - Analyzing: Compare and contrast the different states of matter and analyze the effects of temperature and pressure on their behavior.
- Level 5 - Evaluating: Evaluate the environmental impact of human activities on the matter and propose solutions for reducing waste.
- Level 6 - Creating: Design and conduct an experiment to demonstrate the properties of matter in different states and draw conclusions from the data.

ppp

Topic: Solar System

- Level 1 - Remembering: Recall the names and order of the planets in our solar system and other celestial bodies.
- Level 2 - Understanding: Explain the characteristics and physical properties of the planets and other celestial bodies in our solar system.
- Level 3 - Applying: Use the knowledge of the solar system to predict the position and movement of celestial bodies.
- Level 4 - Analyzing: Analyze the patterns and relationships in the movement of celestial bodies and describe the effects of gravitational forces.
- Level 5 - Evaluating: Evaluate the impact of space exploration on our understanding of the solar system and its potential for future exploration.
- Level 6 - Creating: Design a model of the solar system that demonstrates the relative size and distance of the planets and other celestial bodies.

ᐅᐅᐅ

End Note

In conclusion, **"Creative Connections: Using Art to Explore Science in Primary Classroom"** is a book that seeks to revolutionize science education by integrating art-based activities. By providing teachers with a range of hands-on, interactive activities, this book aims to make science learning more accessible, engaging, and fun for young learners.

Through this book, I hope to inspire teachers to explore the exciting possibilities of integrating art and science in their classrooms and help them create a learning environment that encourages scientific thinking, creativity, and innovation.

I believe that science is not just a subject to be taught but a way of exploring the world around us, and by integrating art into science education, we can help young learners develop a love for science and a lifelong curiosity about the world around them.

I would like to express my gratitude to all the educators who are committed to making science education more accessible and enjoyable for their students. I hope this book serves as a valuable resource for them and inspires them to continue exploring new and innovative ways of teaching science.

Finally, I would like to thank all the readers for taking the time to read this book. I hope you found it informative and helpful in your pursuit of science education.